Designing and Implementing a Professional Development Programme

Jonathan Ellams

CAMBRIDGE
UNIVERSITY PRESS

CAMBRIDGE
UNIVERSITY PRESS

University Printing House, Cambridge CB2 8BS, United Kingdom

One Liberty Plaza, 20th Floor, New York, NY 10006, USA

477 Williamstown Road, Port Melbourne, VIC 3207, Australia

314–321, 3rd Floor, Plot 3, Splendor Forum, Jasola District Centre, New Delhi – 110025, India

79 Anson Road, #06–04/06, Singapore 079906

Cambridge University Press is part of the University of Cambridge.

It furthers the University's mission by disseminating knowledge in the pursuit of education, learning and research at the highest international levels of excellence.

www.cambridge.org
Information on this title: www.cambridge.org/9781108440820

© Cambridge University Press 2018

First published 2018

20 19 18 17 16 15 14 13 12 11 10 9 8 7 6 5 4 3 2 1

Printed and bound in Great Britain by CPI Group (UK) Ltd, Croydon CR0 4YY

A catalogue record for this publication is available from the British Library

ISBN 978-1-10844082-0 Paperback

Contents

How to use this book

WHY USE THIS TEXT?

Developing your own teachers so that they live, breathe and deliver excellence in the classroom is the most powerful thing you can do to impact on the lives of the young people in your care. Success will come from growing your own in-house talent through continuing professional learning. Many Professional Development programmes either focus on theory at the expense of practice, or promise a 'quick fix' that, without being tied to a coherent strategy within your school, is unable to deliver in the long term. This book will allow you to build your own ongoing programme, specific to the needs of your own school, or give you the tools to adapt an external programme so that it feeds into and supports the culture of your institution rather than serving as a short-term solution.

The text will offer a range of ideas and initiatives to achieve this, and will guide you through implementation. It will conclude with three different case studies to show you how other institutions have responded to the challenge you are now facing. Ultimately, this text will provide you with the equipment you need to maximise your chances of launching a Professional Development programme successfully within your school or institution.

HOW CAN THIS TEXT BE USED?

Bringing about a change in culture by implementing a new initiative school-wide requires you to follow certain key steps. Each chapter addresses a stage in bringing about a successful Professional Development programme. For those at the beginning of the journey, every chapter will have something to offer. Those at different stages will be able to dip in and out at different points, referring back if need be.

The book is divided into four clear sections, each of which represents a different stage in the development of your programme. Chapter One will give you the basic framework for setting up your programme, Chapter Two will show you how to negotiate the barriers you will need to overcome in order to achieve successful implementation of your programme, Chapter Three will look at the types of programme available to you in more detail and Chapter Four will show you how to assess the impact of the programme once you have set it in motion. Finally, Chapter Five will show you these methods in practice through a real-life case study.

CHAPTER SUMMARY

Chapter One: *First Steps* will outline exactly how to begin the process. It will ask you to consider your own institution in terms of your planned Professional Development programme. It will challenge you to consider staff perception of Professional Development and the extent to which they engage with it. It will explore how to bring about a change in culture around Professional Development and how to enthuse your staff. It will take you through seven basic steps that will frame the build-up to the launch of your programme: identifying your goal; building a picture of your school; considering when and how to implement your programme; understanding your budget; engaging others; thinking about teacher rewards; and, finally, preparing for launch.

Chapter Two: *Breaking Down Barriers* will look at the barriers that you will need to overcome in order to implement your Professional Development programme and bring about change. The chapter will look at teacher motivation and engagement, effective communication strategies, how to identify the core principles of your institution and the importance of gauging impact. It will also touch on the scale of your initiative, and the role of participation to ensure cooperation and engagement.

Chapter Three: *Professional Development Models* looks at core Professional Development models and how to implement and/or adapt them as you design your own programme. This includes the free-flowing benefits of in-school coaching, the more prescriptive approach of taught Professional Development, and the Japanese concept of 'Lesson Study', the improvement of teaching through research. It also looks at the issue of time, and the practice of lesson observation as a tool in successfully supporting the implementation of your Professional Development model.

Chapter Four: *Measuring Success* looks at how to assess the impact of your Professional Development programme in terms of student outcomes, and how to make sure that it is delivering on the aims you set out at the beginning of the process. The chapter introduces the Kirkpatrick model, a four-tier framework for evaluating the success of training, and looks in detail at the use of portfolios, lesson observations, focus groups and student surveys.

Chapter Five: *Real-World Example – Parkside Federation Academies* provides a detailed example of a Professional Development model in action, giving you a chance to see how the ideas discussed in this book translate into practice 'on the ground'.

Introduction

WHY FOCUS ON PROFESSIONAL DEVELOPMENT?

Research evidence is clear that the most important action that a school can take to improve outcomes for students is to develop their teachers to be more effective, and the most reliable way to achieve this is to create a culture of ongoing professional learning, where teachers are continually developing, adapting and refining their skills and methods.

In 2007, a report entitled *How the World's Best-Performing School Systems Come Out on Top* was published in the UK. It examined current research and explored the different approaches to Professional Development in a number of countries. The authors of the report saw a clear correlation between improvements in outcomes and the status and approach to Professional Development that countries had adopted. In other words, effective Professional Development appeared to hold the key to driving improvement.

Essentially, the report confirmed that if teachers are effectively engaged to develop and improve, then classroom practice, learning and teaching will also improve, in turn driving greater outcomes. Whilst this may on the surface seem a simple equation, it is common sense that developing better teachers should be the highest priority for anyone charged with improving student outcomes. One South Korean policymaker quoted in the report put it simply:

"

The quality of an education system cannot exceed the quality of its teachers.[1]

"

Nevertheless, understanding this in itself is not suddenly going to improve teaching. Schools need to build in sufficient time for teachers to

---

1   Interview, South Korea, 2007, quoted in Barber, B. and Mourshed, M. (2007). *How the world's best-performing school systems come out on top*. McKinsey.

engage in activities, whichever form their Professional Development programme may take. Like most professions, sports or indeed most hobbies, improvement comes with practice, incremental changes, and time to implement and embed. Just as sports people commit to continuous improvement and 'putting in the hours' to find success, so outstanding teachers must commit to long-term development and need to be offered more than just a one-off training course.

Initial teacher training prepares teachers to meet the minimum standards required in the district or country in which they train to teach. Without a focus on Professional Development, this can mark the end of the teacher's supported development; after that, essentially they are on their own. In schools without a culture of continuous professional development, this can translate into teachers who are several years into their teaching careers, yet still only meeting minimum standards. Research and practice around the world repeatedly reinforces the fact that in order to elevate teachers to meet their full potential, ongoing Professional Development is key.

THE BIG PICTURE

According to Pearson's *Global Education Index*, four of the five best education systems in the world are in Asia:

1. South Korea
2. Japan
3. Singapore
4. Hong Kong
5. Finland

The success of Asian education systems has triggered a global spotlight on the continent as researchers, policymakers and educators search for the elusive 'elixir' of education. But, in reality, you don't have to delve too deeply to find out why these countries are so successful. At the heart of their success is a clear investment in Professional Development in every sense.

In 2006, Singapore's Ministry of Education invested $250 million in their GROW model, the **G**rowth of Education Officers, through better **R**ecognition, **O**pportunities, and seeing to their **W**ellbeing. This included enhanced sabbatical opportunities for teachers to give them time to undertake purposeful professional development. Under the scheme, teachers with at least six years of service can take half-pay leave to recharge and renew themselves. A teacher who has had at least 12 years of experience can take up to two and a half months of full-pay leave. Teachers are entitled to claim between $400 and $700 per year for any learning-related expenses that they chose.

Most importantly, every school has a School Staff Developer (SSD), a senior member of staff whose job is to ensure that Training and Professional Development programmes are customised to their teacher's needs, while supporting the school's goals. On top of this, a new Teacher Development Centre has been built to serve as a focal point for the Professional Development of teachers.[2] This investment in Professional Development has no doubt been key in cementing Singapore's place in the top five global education systems.

With South Korea, Japan and Singapore leading the way, it is clear that there is a rethink around the importance of Professional Development occurring around the world. *New Professional Development Standards* were published in the UK in July 2016. The Preamble to these standards is clear:

"

High-quality Professional Development requires workplaces to be steeped in rigorous scholarship, with professionals continually developing and supporting each other so that pupils benefit from the best possible teaching. The design of high-quality Professional Development is as complex a discipline as the design of high-quality teaching. It requires the planning of programmes of connected activities with clarity about intended outcomes, and evaluation.[3]

"

Publishing these standards clearly marks a change in approach to Professional Development in UK schools, raising its status and challenging schools to be creative in their approach.

For the UK, this is a case of 'better late than never'. Levels of recruitment into teacher training in the UK in recent years have dropped while the numbers of people leaving the profession only a

---

2 https://www.britishcouncil.sg/about/press/newsletter-articles/teacher-development; http://www.cdtl.nus.edu.sg/.

3 UK Department of Education (2016). *New Professional Development Standards.*

few years after having trained have risen. Most surveys cite workload and a lack of support as the key reasons for leaving the profession so early on. With only an emergent culture of continuous Professional Development in the majority of UK schools, those that don't leave the profession risk developing little beyond minimal standards. With 30% of UK secondary schools either failing or in need of improvement,[4] the next generation of teachers, having met minimum standards, will find few places to turn for guidance if they wish to develop into outstanding practitioners.

External expertise can be hired. Specialist Leaders of Education (SLEs) – teachers who have been able to prove they have met the standards of outstanding practice – exist to support fellow professionals and can be engaged by schools. The difficulty is that SLE time is charged to schools at £450 a day (as of writing), and with recent research showing that '21,000 teachers are employed in schools with zero or near-zero PD budget ... and the median spend on PD [is] at 0.7% of the school's overall budget,'[5] engaging an SLE for a day, let alone long-term, is not an option for many. In this context, the *New Professional Development Standards* can be seen as an opportunity for positive change that will require new ways of thinking about cost-effective implementation of ongoing Professional Development.

Large-scale change is also occuring in the United States. The US Department of Education recently stated that:

"

Nearly half of $3.0 billion in federal funding ... and billions more in other federal funds goes to the Professional Development of teachers and leaders in our schools ... key investments in infrastructure and data will help to support [new] models and can have long term impact.[6]

"

The US Department of Education has recognised that efforts have lagged in this area and that the focus needs to shift. This has triggered changes at US state level with New York state announcing a change

---

4 https://www.standard.co.uk/news/education/200000-pupils-in-england-being-failed-by-secondary-schools-that-underperform-a3444521.html

5 http://tdtrust.org/benchmarking

6 https://www.ed.gov/oii-news/teacher-professional-and-career-development

in their approach to professional development, replacing their current system with new *Continuing Teacher and Leader Education (CTLE) Requirements* in July 2016. Their ultimate aim is to:

———————————— *"* ————————————

increase the capacity of teachers and teaching assistants to enable and assist all students to higher academic achievement.

———————————— *"* ————————————

NYS Department of Education lays out a number of aims, not least of which are that:

• Professional Development activities/experiences should respond to student achievement data.

• Professional Development should be shaped by teaching staff needs, as evidenced by such data as aggregate results of annual professional performance reviews.

In other words, the Professional Development planning process should be dynamic, reflecting teaching staff and student performance benchmarks of increasing rigour as skill levels are attained.

With a new focus on the value of effective teacher Professional Development around the world, what is needed now is direction. This text offers guidance as to how to approach Professional Development within your own educational setting – how to create a programme that is effective and not just interesting, but appropriate to your institution and focused on improving student outcomes.

1   First steps

....

This section will look at the first steps you need to take to implement a successful Professional Development **programme. The process will be discussed step by step so you will be able to follow every stage, should you need to. If you are at a different stage of developing your programme, move to the next chapter or choose whichever section suits you best.**

....

WHAT TO CONSIDER BEFORE YOU START

You are about to launch an initiative that research, and indeed common sense, shows should have the single biggest impact on learning and teaching in your school and therefore the single biggest impact on student outcomes. You are, however, challenging teachers to be better at teaching and so your new initiative, what you say and do, how it is launched and delivered, and what you ask of your teachers, will be in the spotlight from the outset. This may sound dramatic and even daunting, but it should serve only to inform your approach. As with anything, if what you develop and deliver is of quality, success is likely to follow.

Understanding the value of teaching

The value placed on teaching and teachers varies greatly around the world. You should be best placed to know the state of things in your country and your district, but if you are not, before you begin you should pause to consider the perception of teachers and teaching in your own context, and indeed teachers' own perceptions of their profession. This in itself raises the question of whether teaching is actually seen as a profession in your country, whether teachers are held in high regard or whether they are seen as the root of a problem in education.

It can be hard for teachers to manage the pressure put on them by reforms and initiatives designed to improve performance. Countless educational reforms have come and gone over the years that promise to 'solve the education problem'. Such discussions often avoid external factors such as the impact of changes in society, new technologies, poverty and the changing nature of family structures, and instead tend to lay blame firmly at the feet of teachers themselves. This can be dispiriting, but in order to proceed with an effective Professional Development programme, you will need to put such concerns to one side and focus on your role in encouraging the *profession* to change, adapt and improve, since this is how you will personally be achieving impact.

Confronting barriers to change

Depending on your context, you may also be concerned that your teachers might themselves not want to change their practice, that they may be happy to continue to teach in the way that they are used to, or indeed as they believe teachers have always done. If so, reassure yourself that evidence shows that with the right approach and the right resources, teachers can change, adapt and improve their teaching (see the **Introduction**).

As you have been charged with creating, developing or improving teaching within your institution through Professional Development, you have an amazing opportunity ahead of you. The following steps will take you through the planning process you need to undertake to bring that opportunity to life, introducing you to ideas that will be explored in more detail in **Chapters Two** to **Four**:

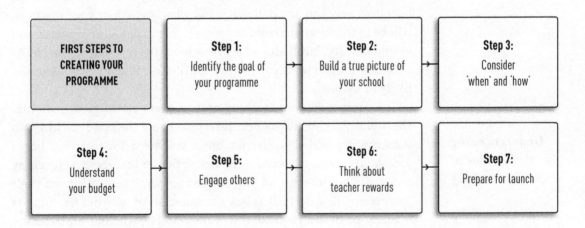

If you use this framework as a guide, you will ensure that when the time arrives for you to launch your Professional Development programme, you are ready and prepared. Let us look at each step in more detail.

■ STEP ONE: **IDENTIFY THE GOAL OF YOUR PROGRAMME**

First, you must consider exactly what you want your Professional Development programme to do. The core aims of Professional Development should be to strive to:

The core aims of Professional Development

- **improve learning and teaching**, and therefore
- **improve student outcomes**

This may sound obvious, but it is not uncommon for institutions to overlook this aim and, in doing so, fail to make the fundamental link between Professional Development and student outcomes. With this in mind, now consider:

1. How will your programme achieve **classroom impact**?

If you overlook this, even if you are following the latest research or advice, you could still end up implementing a programme that has little consideration for the actual needs of your institution, teachers and students. Professional Development that is not targeted to the specific needs of the classroom will be *interesting* at best, but will deliver few practical day-to-day results.

Realising the importance of classroom practice

There are many ways to ensure your Professional Development programme delivers change in the classroom, including recognised models – lesson study, coaching in triad peer groups and taught sessions, for example – all of which will be discussed in more detail in **Chapter Three:** *Professional Development Models*. Each method will suit some institutions more than others. You need to work out what is right in your context.

Whilst any number of tweaks and improvements can be made within any and every school, classroom practice should always receive the greatest attention. Every teacher can improve their teaching and it is the duty of every school to create an environment in which teaching and learning can improve.

Next, consider:

2. How will your programme foster **collaboration**?

The value of sharing ideas

Although this is not a core aim, collaboration is an ancillary benefit to any effective Professional Development initiative. Professional Development should bring staff together from across faculties and departments, affording opportunities to share ideas and resources, and build a more cohesive curriculum. Collaborative Professional

Development also gives countless opportunities to involve staff in the delivery of Professional Development and therefore engage in research.

Addressing the above points will ensure your programme has a solid basis. A good idea is to write a *mission statement* to help you to visualise it.

Writing a mission statement:

It is a good idea to write a mission statement to identifiy an initial set of criteria for your programme:

- Through this initiative I aim to ...
- My best-case scenario would be ...

You could tie your mission statement to concrete, measurable goals, for example:

- Through this initiative I aim to make learning and teaching outstanding across the school.
- My best-case scenario would be to see pupil results in the top 10% nationally.

Or you may wish your mission statement to reflect more subtle goals:
- Through this initiative I aim to invigorate staff and remind them why they entered teaching.
- My best-case scenario would be a happier, more engaged staff who spend more time talking about learning and teaching, and less time complaining about students.

Whatever your approach, remember to revisit, revise and rewrite them as you go BUT never over the top of the previous statements. Allow these statements to chart your journey and therefore inform your next steps by allowing you to learn from past mistakes, misconceptions and changing ideas.

■ STEP TWO: BUILD A TRUE PICTURE OF YOUR SCHOOL

In order to know how best to approach Professional Development in your institution, you must build a true and realistic picture of how your institution and your staff currently operate in terms of teaching and learning.

Do not rely on what you think you know: you will get best results if you explore every possible avenue to build your true picture of the *strengths* and *weaknesses* within your school. One way to approach the process is to treat it like a lesson.

Look at strengths and weaknesses

Using the 'classroom analogy'

When taking on a new class, a teacher usually begins by examining any data or information they hold on the students in order to inform their approach to teaching that class. For example, the teacher might consider:

- What is their prior attainment?
- What are their target grades?
- Do they have specific needs?

In order for your programme to be successful, you must think about your school in the same way. If you keep to this analogy of the classroom as a guide to approaching devising your new initiative, you will not go far wrong. Use the following diagram to frame your ideas:

Figure 1: *Building a true picture of your school in terms of teaching and learning*

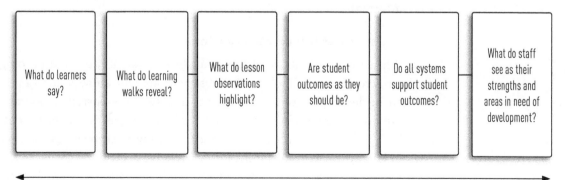

These questions can be approached in any order. It is not an exhaustive list and you may be able to ask further questions specific to your school that will better inform your approach. Let's look in more detail at how to act on these six questions:

1. Listen to learners

This could entail directly interviewing learners. Remember, you need to get staff on-side and such actions could be viewed as hostile, so be considered in your approach. Engaging with students more softly may also elicit more information, remove any misconceptions that can come out of student interviews and allow students themselves to be more honest and open with their views.

Realise the value of student opinion

2. Go on learning walks

Whether formal or informal, learning walks create an opportunity to go in and out of lessons. Learning walks are essentially short lesson visits where you can get a *feel* for the lesson, rather than carrying out a full observation. Whilst it does just give a flavour, it allows you to visit a number of lessons in a short space of time. During a learning walk, ask:

- Are all students engaged?
- Is the teacher leading from the front?
- How is the room laid out?
- Are clear instructions given?
- Are tasks time-based?

Spending just five minutes in a classroom can deliver a wealth of information.

3. Carry out lesson observations

While learning walks will give you a broad insight into what is going on across your school, lesson observations will allow you to build an in-depth picture of how classes and teachers currently operate. Providing lesson observation pro formas (templates for document-ing your observations) are detailed, looking back over the history of lesson observations will be an invaluable activity. What were the strengths of each lesson and what would have made the lesson better?

4. Look at student outcomes

Really dig down into student outcomes to find patterns. For example:

- Is there a gender bias?
- Did those with specific needs perform relatively well?
- Did vocational subjects outperform more traditionally academic subjects?

Identify drivers of success

Ask what is currently working well to drive success as well as what might be holding things back.

5. Look at systems that support student outcomes

All systems should either directly or indirectly support student outcomes, learning and teaching, but this is not always the case. Examine what systems you have in place to monitor and improve student attendance and behaviour, and the day-to-day role of the teacher. Professional Development is not just for classroom teachers; support staff who create and run school systems need support and development too.

6. Survey your staff

Your programme must be personalised. Whilst you are the one who needs to make final decisions about your provision, allowing teachers to identify their own strengths and areas in need of development is extremely powerful. When fear of judgement is removed, people are usually very honest about their abilities.

Removing fear of judgement

You may find it easier to tackle these questions and get better results if you form a *working party*.

Tip: Form a working party

Involving others from the start is invaluable in terms of getting a true picture of your institution, so form a working party or research group.

Carefully consider the **name** you give this group. This might sound like an insignificant detail, but it is important as you will be setting a tone with all you do. A 'research group' will have different connotations to a 'working party'.

There are a number of methods that can be used to identify where change is needed and potential barriers to that change. Your choice of method should be guided by local circumstances, including the numbers of professionals involved and the time and resources available.

One way is to identify key individuals you can work with to help develop your programme:

Involving key individuals

- Talk to individuals who have a specific understanding of a given situation and have the knowledge, skills and authority to enable them to think around a topic and explore new ideas.
- Allow these key individuals to feed into your ideas and your planning.
- Consider talking to a group of key individuals during one of their regular meetings – for example, Heads of Department.
- If you wish, call meetings independent of your usual calendared meetings, but make sure you are transparent about such meetings.

This method has a number of advantages, for example:

- it enables ideas to be explored in a collaborative fashion
- detailed information can be obtained
- it is quick and inexpensive.

There may be some disadvantages, for example:

- it relies heavily on the key individuals
- their responses may be subject to bias
- it may be difficult to find the right people to talk to.

Weigh up these advantages and disadvantages, and tailor the action you take accordingly.

Once you have a true and clear picture of your school in terms of teaching and learning, you can begin to consider what Professional Development model (or models) will work best for your institution and staff. It can be very helpful to write up what you find rather than trying to keep all of your discoveries in your head. One way to do this is by writing up your thoughts as if they are part of a *presentation*. Try this exercise using the guidelines opposite. Obviously these questions and your answers are for your eyes only but, if answered honestly, they will give you a very good picture of your institution.

Exercise: *Prepare a presentation*

Imagine you have to give a presentation during which you summarise your school or group of schools.

Write up your presentation using the following questions to guide your thoughts.

- WHAT TYPE OF STAFF DO YOU HAVE? ARE THEY WILLING TO TRY NEW THINGS AND INNOVATE? ARE THEY FRIENDLY? APPROACHABLE? DO THEY SOCIALISE OR FINISH WORK AND GO HOME?

- HOW WELL DO STAFF WORK TOGETHER? IN FRIENDSHIP GROUPS? AT DEPARTMENT LEVEL? FACULTY LEVEL? WHOLE SCHOOL?

- WHAT PERCENTAGE OF LESSONS ARE GOOD OR OUTSTANDING?

- WHICH SUBJECT AREAS ARE MOST ENJOYED BY STUDENTS?

- WHICH SUBJECT AREAS WOULD YOU MOST LIKE TO LEARN IN? WHY?

- HOW MANY LESSONS ARE STUDENTS ACTIVE IN?

- WHICH SUBJECT AREAS GET THE HIGHEST STUDENT OUTCOMES?

- WHICH SUBJECT AREAS ARE BEST AT ENGAGING BOYS? GIRLS? DISAFFECTED STUDENTS?

- IS THERE A GOOD RELATIONSHIP BETWEEN SUPPORT STAFF AND TEACHERS? TEACHERS AND MIDDLE LEADERS? TEACHERS AND SENIOR LEADERS? MIDDLE LEADERS AND SENIOR LEADERS?

- ARE YOUR SENIOR TEAM OFTEN AROUND SCHOOL? ARE THEY OFTEN IN LESSONS? IF THEY ARE, ARE THEY WARMLY WELCOMED BY STAFF?

- DO SUPPORT STAFF HELP THE TEACHERS THEY LIKE BEST OR DO THE SYSTEMS GENUINELY WORK TO SUPPORT STAFF?

- HOW WERE YOUR LEARNING WALKS GREETED BY DIFFERENT TEACHERS?

- DO YOU FEEL YOU HAVE A GENUINE OPEN-DOOR POLICY OR ARE PEOPLE FRIGHTENED BY THE IDEA OF OBSERVATIONS?

- ARE SOME TEACHERS MORE STRICT THAN OTHERS?

- WHAT IS BEHAVIOUR LIKE IN YOUR SCHOOL?

- WOULD YOU SEND YOUR CHILDREN TO THE SCHOOL?

- WOULD YOU BE HAPPY IF YOUR CHILDREN WERE TAUGHT BY TEACHER X OR Y?

This piece of writing, informed by these suggested questions, will be invaluable. It will inform the type of Professional Development you introduce, the way you launch your initiative, and how you might affect the culture within your school as well as improve outcomes. Do not forget to refer back to this document at each stage: there is a difference between *your perceptions* of your institution and the *reality* of your institution.

■ STEP THREE: **CONSIDER 'WHEN AND HOW'**

Now you need to decide when you are going to launch your new initiative and in what way. Ultimately, you have two options:

1. Build your picture, devise a plan and *then* share this with your staff, or

2. Be honest from the outset: state that there is going to be a new approach to Professional Development but that you do not know yet what it is going to look like.

Look at past initiatives

If you adopt the second approach, some staff will find security in your honesty and it may start by introducing the notion of collaboration, but others might feel it shows you are ill-equipped. There is no universal right or wrong answer here, just the right or wrong answer for your institution, and only you can know your institution. Consider previous initiative launches – what did your staff respond to best?

■ STEP FOUR: **UNDERSTAND YOUR BUDGET**

Now is a good time to introduce the notion of cost. Consider:

1. How much of your budget will you assign to your programme?

The cost of outside experts

With every decision that you make about your Professional Development programme, you must think about the cost implication and how that will affect the budget available to you. You might conclude that you would like outside experts to deliver bespoke courses, for example, in which case you will have to ask if this is affordable for you. Who makes the final decision? You might need to discuss your ideas with your business manager or accounts department before you can include them as part of your programme.

2. Are you aware of *hidden* costs?

If you decide to engage outside experts to assist with the implementation of your programme, ensure you have asked about *full* costs so no hidden surprises catch you out. For example, a lot of outside providers charge administration fees for certification. Some higher education establishments charge for converting degree points in order for them to be applied to their courses.

Other decisions will have time implications that indirectly impact on cost. You may decide that staff working in triads or groups would work for you, but will this time be timetabled? If so, can this be achieved?

Timetabling and cover costs

One of the largest costs often not factored into budgets is cover costs to allow teachers off-timetable to engage with courses. Such costs can soon get out of hand if not planned in advance. (**Chapter Two:** *Breaking Down Barriers* will go into more detail about time, cost and other factors around external providers, and **Chapter Three:** *Professional Development Models* will discuss devising programmes with time costs in mind.)

3. Have you spoken to staff and leaders?

Now is the time for some tentative conversations, be it with your staff as a pre-launch or with your executive body or senior leaders, in terms of:

- costing
- implementation, and
- desired outcomes.

You have a balancing act ahead of you when it comes to discussing cost with your colleagues. You will need a budget and so must alert your financial manager, but at this stage you won't know exactly how much you will need. Like any large-scale initiative, you need to propose your idea and you will need to cost any financial implications as best you can.

Engaging your staff and leaders is an essential early step in developing your thoughts around your programme, and is worth now looking at in more detail.

■ STEP FIVE: **ENGAGE OTHERS**

Research shows that Professional Development is most effective when it fully involves leaders from the outset, allowing them to model and champion effective Professional Development at every stage.[1] That said, when considering key figures to engage, you will need to think beyond your senior team and/or finance team.

1. Engage your **teachers**

It is easy to get lost in thinking that once you have sold the idea to an executive team and have had a budget approved you have been successful. Yes, they will be the ones approving your overarching idea(s) and spending plan, but ultimately your programme will be owned by your day-to-day teachers.

You will have to think carefully about this if you are to successfully engage both teachers and senior management, as success will hinge on how you handle both groups during the early stages of your new initiative.

2. Write down your **success criteria** in terms of engagement

What does success look like?

You need to define your idea of success in terms of engagement from the start – an idea of success that goes beyond the higher structures of your organisation. Successful Professional Development develops teaching and therefore improves outcomes however you measure them. This may seem like an obvious thing to say, but sometimes it is possible to lose sight of what it is you want to achieve. In order to avoid this, just as you wrote a mission statement earlier, aside from any proposal you draw up for the boardroom, create a short list of *success criteria* in the area of teacher engagement for yourself, and revisit this often.

3. Think about how you will **promote your programme** to staff

Once you have grasped the idea that, whatever shape your programme is going to take, success will be measured by your teachers, you need to work out how you are going to sell your programme to them.

---

1   UK Dept. of Education (2016). *Standards for teacher's professional development.* www.gov.uk/government/publications/standard-for-teachers-professional-development. UK: Department of Education, 12 July.

Many teachers will have heard many presentations promising vast improvements through the latest Professional Development initiative. Your teachers may have been made to take part in any number of initiatives, some successful, some less so. Some of your teachers will be new to the profession and will be hugely enthusiastic, but others will have been teaching for some time and may greet any new idea with a level of cynicism. Having already considered a number of ways to build a realistic picture of your institution, it is now time to make use of this information. More detail about how to go about this can be found in **Chapter Two:** *Breaking Down Barriers* in the sections on *motivation* and your *communication strategy*.

4. Build a **realistic picture** of staff enthusiasm for change

You will benefit from building a realistic picture of your staff in terms of how enthusiastically they will greet your plans.

Buy-in from all

Regardless of how your programme is introduced and the model of involvement you will create, Professional Development programmes will invariably seek engagement from the whole institution and will therefore need to be introduced sensitively. You will find this easier with a basic understanding of *group dynamics* and how they work (see below).

Group dynamics

Psychologist Bruce Tuckman wrote a lot about the dynamics of a group and how to successfully bring people together.

He stated that in a state of change a group would go through four stages:

1. Forming: At this stage there will be a mix of emotions greeting a new initiative: anxiety, excitement, positivity, cynicism. It is vital that any new initiative is led well at this early stage and that you pay close attention to any key figures emerging.

2. Storming: This is the most challenging stage for you to manage. Conflict and frustration may become evident and you must act quickly to calm any nerves, dispel any myths and challenge any nay sayers/blockers.

>

3. Norming: At this stage people should be seeing value in what you have put in place. People should be working together and starting to see real benefit from your new programme.

4. Performing: By now there should be collaborative working, with those involved seeing success as a predominant factor in your programme. All systems in place should be effective enough to deal with new members of the group joining or indeed others leaving.

In terms of the dynamics within any group, any new initiative will be greeted in a number of different ways by different people. There will be key figures within your institutions who have real influence over others. Such individuals can be a force for good, but equally they can be a force for bad. You must work out who these individuals are and what motivates them.

Remember, you are the gatekeeper for your initiative. You must have your ear to the ground, constantly testing to ensure that you have consensus and are working to resolve any barriers that may emerge (see **Chapter Two:** *Breaking Down Barriers* for more detail on what to look out for). Any form of change in any institution will be greeted in a number of different and sometimes conflicting ways; schools may deal in the education of children, but this does not mean things are straightforward – as institutions they are as complex as any.

Confronting cynicism

You must be prepared to face cynicism from some who are quite happy to be 'good enough' and have no desire to constantly strive for excellence. Whilst the profession often talks of 'outstanding teaching', and often presents meeting minimum standards as a sign of failure, it is important to remember that meeting those standards is enough for some. There are also those who would say that constantly striving for excellence is damaging to the profession. Do not just dismiss such views as it could be argued they are valid. It may be that such views are held by people who feel let down by the profession, have seen many failed initiatives come and go, or have given many good years to teaching and have been tired by it. Your job is to get as many people on-side as is possible, and you have a duty to support and help all your staff in whichever way is best for your institution and for them.

> ## Pause for thought
>
> Now might be a good point for your first review of your original *aims* and *mission statement* and add to and/or make some revisions. It is also a good idea to write out what you have achieved so far. This can inform your next steps.

Planning checklist:

I HAVE:

☐ CONSIDERED WHAT I WANT MY PROGRAMME TO ACHIEVE

☐ WRITTEN OUT AIMS, OBJECTIVES AND A MISSION STATEMENT

☐ BUILT A TRUE AND THOROUGH PICTURE OF MY SCHOOL(S) THROUGH:

  ☐ LEARNING WALKS

  ☐ CONVERSATIONS WITH STUDENTS AND STAFF

  ☐ LOOKING BACK OVER LESSON OBSERVATIONS

  ☐ LOOKING CLOSELY AT STUDENT OUTCOMES

  ☐ SURVEYING MY STAFF

☐ ANSWERED THE QUESTIONS ABOUT MY SCHOOL(S) WITH COMPLETE HONESTY

☐ WRITTEN A SHORT SUMMARY OF MY SCHOOL AND STAFF

☐ BEGUN TO CONSIDER COSTS

☐ CONSIDERED WHO MY KEY STAFF ARE AND HOW TO ENGAGE THEM

■ STEP SIX: **THINK ABOUT TEACHER REWARDS**

You have built a picture of your school, and you now understand the way your staff operate and are clear that you need to engage with them from the start. Simply understanding how to get the attention of your teachers will not be enough, however. You need to think about ongoing engagement, and to do this you need to understand the value of rewards.

Selling initiative value

From the very beginning you must convince your staff of the value of your initiative and so must convince them that they will be rewarded for their efforts. This may be a case of making staff aware of rewards that will come their way as a natural result of their efforts, such as:

• improved outcomes

• better lessons

• decreased workload

• a happier work environment

• increased job satisfaction.

You must be clear that different staff will want different rewards from each other and from you, and you should be aware of this as you tailor your engagement with teachers to make them aware of these different rewards.

As well as these automatic rewards, you might want to think about a more tangible reward for teacher commitment:

• increased wages

Ask yourself, *is progression through your Professional Development programme going to be linked to your appraisal system and therefore your pay policy?* In this area, as with others, you must be clear in order to avoid creating any confusion which could risk disillusioning those you are trying to reward.

Teacher awareness of change

Making your staff aware of the rewards they can look forward to might sound like the easy part, but it is not as straightforward as it sounds and will require careful preparation. Do not lose sight of the fact that you are asking people to consider their practice and to improve, which carries with it the implication that they *need* to improve. You must reinforce the idea that teachers should *want* to constantly improve and add to their skills base, and that this is a reward in itself. Your teachers need to be aware of the implicit and explicit rewards of their professional development, and must be encouraged to believe in them.

STEP 7: **PREPARE FOR LAUNCH**

You have only one attempt at launch, one attempt to get buy-in from your staff. If things go wrong, cause problems, or make more problems than are solved, then your initiative, and to some extent you, could gather negative energy which will be hard to shake off. Effective preparation for launch is essential, so it is important to think about it now.

At this stage you are unlikely to have decided upon your programme – this is covered in **Chapter Three:** *Professional Development Models* – but it is important to touch on the launch at this stage as technically you have already begun. Even if you have not uttered a word to anyone about your potential ideas, the fact that you have begun the process means your programme has already undergone a 'launch' of sorts. Be mindful of this fact. People will feel change underfoot as an unconscious process which can be both exciting and unnerving.

Using the 'iceberg metaphor'

Look at the iceberg metaphor illustrated on the following page as you work through implementation. This metaphor works for so many aspects of your current work. It serves as a metaphor for the culture of your institution, and for the emotions of those therein – only a small percentage of what is being felt will be visible. It should serve as a metaphor for the launch process and indeed implementation of the programme as a whole. The launch and roll-out of the programme itself sits above the water, clear for all to see, but below lie the concerns of those affected by the change. These concerns may not be visible, but you must remember that they exist all the same.

If you are able to think about your institution and its receptiveness to change in this way, you can understand the decisions that follow with a deeper picture in your mind of the impact they might make both above and below the surface.

Figure 2: *The iceberg metaphor*

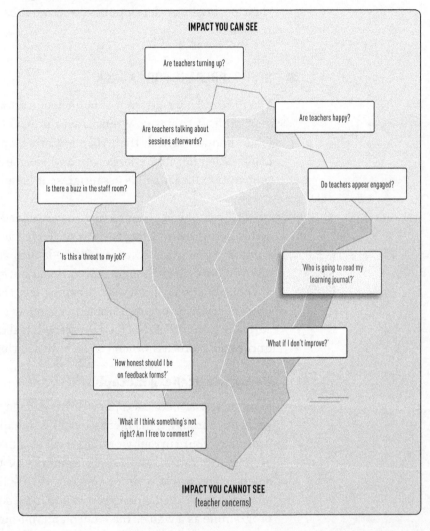

In order to ensure that your launch goes smoothly, make sure you have thought about the following decisions and worked them into your plan for implementation:

1. Decide how to formally announce the launch of your programme

When officially launching any new initiative, you need to afford it the status it deserves. How and when you launch sets the status of your initiative, and so you must consider in detail the tone you want to set.

2. Work out the order and stages of programme implementation

You will need to decide the precise order in which you intend to launch your programme. It may help to plan out your launch step-by-step as this will highlight any potential problems you may need to pre-empt.

3. Think about the scale of your institution(s)

Are you looking at more than one school?

The size and make-up of your institution will impact on your plans from a purely logistical perspective. If you are a relatively small institution in terms of staff numbers, there will be less to consider than institutions with, say, a hundred staff, and less again than a multi-site network of schools. This also raises questions about what you develop in terms of the various needs of each institution. Yes, all schools can improve learning and teaching regardless of their current strength, but *how* can differ.

If you are rolling out your programme across more than one school, you will need to decide how you are going to achieve this. Do you have staff meetings or staff conferences across the schools?

4. Think about the scale of roll-out for your programme

The scale of programme roll-out may or may not be dictated by the scale of your institution, but you must think about it in advance. Ultimately, you have two options that will shape roll-out. Will you:

- initiate your programme in full from the start, or
- pilot each aspect one piece at a time?

Communicating your investment

Like most things, there are benefits to both approaches. By rolling out 'full-on' you communicate fully the size of the investment you are making in your staff. It allows everybody to see precisely what is on offer and allows your programme to begin impacting fully from the outset. Conversely, by piloting your programme piece-by-piece, involving some key members of staff as you go, you will be able to adapt and personalise your programme. You can also take the temperature of your staff in terms of how they react to the offer.

CHECKLIST FOR YOUR LAUNCH:

Use the checklist on the following page to help make sure your launch is a success:

Launch checklist:

- [ ] CONSIDER THE NEEDS OF YOUR INSTITUTIONS
- [ ] WHAT NEEDS TO CHANGE?
- [ ] WHAT PREVIOUS ATTEMPTS AT CHANGE HAVE SUCCEEDED?
- [ ] WHY DID IT/THEY SUCCEED?
- [ ] WHAT PREVIOUS ATTEMPTS AT CHANGE HAVE BEEN TRIALLED AND FAILED?
- [ ] WHY DID IT/THEY FAIL?
- [ ] CONSIDER THE OUTCOME(S) YOU WANT TO DRIVE FOR
- [ ] ASCERTAIN RESOURCES AVAILABLE - HOW MUCH TIME? HOW MUCH MONEY?
- [ ] ASCERTAIN THE LEVEL OF COMMITMENT FROM SENIOR STAFF/ EXECUTIVE BOARD
- [ ] RESEARCH PROGRAMMES AVAILABLE - IN HOUSE, EXTERNAL, VERIFIED/CERFICATED
- [ ] PILOT COURSES?
- [ ] PILOT ASPECTS OF EACH COURSE?

The table on the following pages summarises what you should have thought about so far in this chapter as you prepare to set up your programme. These seven outlined steps towards launch have equipped you with a basic framework for your thoughts about initiating your Professional Development programme. The next chapter will turn its attention to some of the barriers you will have to break down in order to turn these initial ideas into reality.

Chapter One summary

This chapter has introduced seven basic steps to preparing for implementation of your Professional Development programme.

1 Identify the goal of your programme
- How will your programme achieve classroom impact?
- How will your programme foster collaboration?
- Write a *mission statement*

2 Build a true picture of your school
- Use the 'classroom analogy'
    Listen to learners
    Go on learning walks
    Carry out lesson observations
    Look at student outcomes
    Look at systems that support student outcomes
    Survey your staff
- Form a working party

3 Consider when and how
Will you build your picture, devise your plan, and then share it with staff, or announce your programme and then work out how to implement it?

4 Understand your budget
- How much will you assign to professional development?
- Are you aware of hidden costs?
- Have you spoken to staff and leaders?

5 Engage others
- Engage your teachers
- Write down your success criteria in terms of engagement
- Build a realistic picture of staff enthusiasm for change
    Understand group dynamics

6 Think about teacher rewards

- Indirect rewards (classroom and teaching benefits)
- Direct rewards (pay implications)

7 Prepare for launch

- Decide how to formally announce your programme
- Work out the order and stages of programme implementation
- Think about the scale of your institution(s)
- Think about the scale of roll-out for your programme
- Use the 'iceberg' metaphor

2 Breaking down barriers

In this section you will begin to explore the early stages of designing your Professional Development **programme. You will find out how to align your programme with your school's core principles and how to overcome the common barriers to change you will encounter in setting up your programme, with a focus on the areas of motivation, communication, impact and scale.**

UNDERSTANDING THE BARRIERS TO CHANGE

To develop a successful strategy for change, you need to understand the types of barriers you will face in your institution. Using this knowledge, you can consider which of those may be relevant to a particular problem. Following careful consideration, it is possible to develop a tailored approach to overcome these barriers, encourage changes in behaviour and, ultimately, implement your programme.

Awareness of what needs to change, and why, is the vital first step in enabling change to occur. Evidence shows that many teaching professionals are unaware of, or lack familiarity with, the latest evidence-based practice.[1] Whilst some teachers will be eager to improve, *What needs to change and why?* others may only be as informed as the last training day they attended, which for some was the day they finished their teacher training. In addition, they may be aware that new research has been published but do not know how their current way of working could be improved as a result. Some longer-term teachers may perceive the latest piece of research to be the latest 'fad', while others may trust the research but feel it undermines their autonomy. Understanding the cause of these

---

1   See Ko, J., Sammons, P. & Bakkum, L. (2015). *Effective Teaching.* Reading: Education Development Trust. https://www.educationdevelopmenttrust.com/~/media/EDT/Reports/Research/2015/r-effective-teaching.pdf; *Times Education Supplement* (2016). Teachers do not have time to learn about research evidence, studies find. https://www.tes.com/news/school-news/breaking-news/teachers-do-not-have-time-learn-about-research-evidence-studies-find

feelings is a necessary part of developing your approach to change in the form of Professional Development.

This chapter will begin by outlining the problems of adopting a 'one-size-fits-all' approach in the face of this diverse workforce, and then look at other barriers to change, and ways to overcome them, in relation to **motivation**, **communication**, **impact**, **core principles** and **scale**. These are the fundamental areas of change you will need to navigate as you move beyond generic third-party offers to develop a truly effective and personal Professional Development programme for your school.

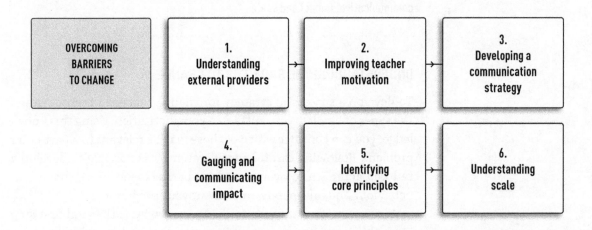

1: UNDERSTANDING EXTERNAL PROVIDERS

As discussed in the **Introduction** and **Chapter One**, the best Professional Development programmes will engage your teachers in *continuing* Professional Development (also known as CPD). Many pre-packaged 'off-the-shelf' training courses do exist, some of which can be available to purchase and/or complete online, and some of which might involve sending your teachers to training events, or even bring-ing in external experts to carry out events at your school. Such pre-packaged options sell themselves as a tempting quick fix. In theory they should allow you to implement Professional Development with the minimum of fuss. However, the decision to rely on courses that promise a one-off, 'one-size-fits-all' solution, rather than ongoing,

Thinking short-term

customised training, has significant pitfalls and could prove to be the greatest barrier to change in your institution.

The problem with outsourcing Professional Development in this way is that trainers deliver their standard training and then disappear. This approach can be superficial; there is no back-up or ongoing communication with teachers and no planned system of evaluation of impact. Not only will this deliver minimal results, it will also impact negatively on teacher motivation.

> **A fair amount of teacher Professional Development (also known variously as teacher training, InSET, CPD or professional learning) is really bad. I don't just mean that it's poor value for money or insufficiently effective – it's much worse than that. A large swathe of training has no effect whatsoever on pupil outcomes.**[2]

Not all external providers fall into this category, and those that offer courses that can be customised in-house can, in fact, provide great benefits to your Professional Development programme (see **Chapter Three:** *Professional Development Models* for details of providers offering customisable courses). When looking at external provision, it is to these courses that you should turn your attention. But remember that even if you can employ a quality provider, it is best not to rely *solely* on outside help; the standard of your Professional Development offer will be determined by the relevance it has to your own context.

If you *are* going to harness external provision, you will need to pay particular attention to the barriers to change that time, cost and access will present to implementation.

Time, cost, access

Time, cost and access are the most frequently cited hurdles to engaging in continuing Professional Development,[3] and while these will

---

2 Weston, D. (2012). How effective is the professional development undertaken by teachers? *The Guardian* online. https://www.theguardian.com/teacher-network/teacher-blog/2012/mar/26/teacher-training-development

3 See Weston, D. (2015). *Developing great teaching: Lessons from the international reviews into effective professional development*. Teacher Development Trust. http://tdtrust.org/about/dgt. For a summary, see http://tdtrust.org/press-release-21000-teachers-schools-reporting-no-cpd-budget-says-teacher-development-trust-study.

present a challenge regardless of the Professional Development route you take, they are particularly relevant if you are considering an off-the-shelf option. It is worth looking at them in more detail.

Even without the demands of Professional Development training, those in the teaching profession face a lot of pressure on their time. The general workload, the responsibility of supporting pupils and the necessity of marking homework, amongst other things, means that the teacher's burden will often spill beyond school hours.

Time |

Professional Development will necessarily take up time either during or outside work hours, both of which will place increased pressure on teachers' already valuable resources. Timetabling Professional Development during work hours will mean taking time away from the other responsibilites that teachers already face. You will want to minimise this impact. Off-the-shelf courses organised during work hours, in particular, are likely to give you and your staff less control over the 'when' and 'how' of their training, causing increased disruption to their workday.

Equally, given that personal demands exist outside of the school environment too, expecting teachers to undertake Professional Development independently (i.e. off-site, through a third party and outside work hours) will exert unreasonable further pressure in most cases and may yield few positive results, no matter how motivated your teachers may be.

Cost |

Cost will be a factor for you and your school as you budget for Professional Development. Off-the-shelf packages come with an inevitable price tag, but also come with further hidden costs. The cost of off-site training could have extra hidden implications, such as the cost of travel, and the cost of covering classes while the teacher is travelling to and from the course.

You may conclude that you could offer training tailored towards specific teacher needs by using off-the-shelf training packages and allowing your teachers the ability to choose which training package suits them. In practice, however, cost concerns could cause your teachers to feel (or indeed be) limited in their training choices to those courses that are deemed affordable, organisationally relevant or institutionally valuable – health and safety, for example. This sort of training is important but should not represent the limit of your teachers' Professional Development options.

Access |

Problems of access can be a direct result of the fact that off-the-shelf courses are not tailored to a specific institution, particularly if those courses require teachers to leave the school environment rather than bringing experts on-site. Many Professional Development courses are organised as one-off events that take place at an external location once or twice a year, causing disruption and logistical problems, while delivering little positive impact. This experience is likely to communicate to your teachers that Professional Development is short-term and ineffective, triggering apathy and fatigue in the face of what should be an exciting learning opportunity.

For schools in rural locations, the issue of access can be even more significant. Travelling to events can in itself be costly, time-consuming and, ultimately, an inefficient way of going about learning.

Not all teachers are the same

Another barrier affecting Professional Development participation that is compounded by the 'one-size-fits-all' approach is the fact that your teacher workforce will be at different career stages, with different skill levels and confidence levels. Each will have a different career or life plan.

In addition to this it is important to remember that, as with any workforce, not all teachers automatically strive to be outstanding. Given the fact that, much like the students themselves, teachers have different learning styles, finding or creating a single programme that can meet the needs of everyone is a difficult task.

Moving beyond 'one-size-fits-all'

We have established that you are not going to 'break down barriers' and bring about change using a 'one-size-fits-all' off-the-shelf package that cannot be personalised. But if you *are* to implement an effective ongoing Professional Development programme that caters to different needs, what issues do you need to consider? Understanding how to navigate the potential barriers to change in the key areas of *motivation*, *communication*, *impact*, *core principles* and *scale* will allow you to tailor Professional Development in your school in a personal, ongoing and effective way that engages your staff and delivers effective results.

■ 2: IMPROVING TEACHER MOTIVATION

Motivation is a fundamental part of nearly everything we do. There are some obvious ways to drive motivation and change behaviour – for example, providing incentives or imposing penalties. But the factors that affect motivation are complex and you will need to think more deeply about them in order to truly understand your workforce. Remember that these factors will vary from one teacher to another.

- **Self-motivation:** Do your teachers have the *drive* and *desire* to improve?

- **Personal beliefs:** How will the personal *beliefs* and *attitudes* of your teachers impact the way they will behave?

- **Openness to the views of others:** Some teachers may find it difficult to accept a new idea or programme if it is in conflict with their current practice or the opinion of an influential colleague. Equally, if a colleague who supports a new programme is held in high esteem, their opinion could enhance teacher motivation.

- **Self-worth:** A person's belief in their own ability to adopt a new behaviour also has an impact on whether a change is implemented.

With these in mind, think about the following questions:

1. How is your programme likely to be perceived?

Motivation and perception

The personal characteristics discussed above will affect an individual's perception of your Professional Development programme, which in turn will dictate their level of motivation. Here lie a number of potential barriers to change.

Unless you frame it otherwise, some teachers will see Professional Development as a top-down process run by school management solely for the benefit of the institution. Participation in Professional Development programmes varies widely from organisation to organisation and, though recognised as important, it is still not always clearly defined in policy or procedures.

It is important to tailor your programme to the needs of staff and make it much more about the personal development of individuals, and not just for the benefit of the organisation. An important step towards achieving this is to ensure that adequate support mechanisms are in place.

2. Does your programme offer the right support?

Asking people to change their practice is a significant request, and individuals need to know not only *what* needs to change, but also *how* best to competently carry out the change.

Support structures

People will need time to learn new skills and practise them, and the time needed will differ from teacher to teacher. It is paramount that you put in place, formally or informally, support from peers such as mentoring or working parties (see also **Chapter One:** *First Steps*). If you are unable to offer this kind of support, motivation will suffer.

The ability of teachers to learn new skills will depend on their:

- individual abilities
- interpersonal skills
- coping strategies.

In order to respond to the needs of individual teachers, you will need to ensure that support is in place that takes into account the fact that abilities, interpersonal skills and coping strategies vary from one teacher to the next.

3. Will your programme be mandatory?

Another key decision that could have a significant impact on motivation is whether you make involvement in your programme mandatory. Compulsory Professional Development is often regarded with some cynicism and could present a barrier to change if it hinders teacher engagement:

- Mandatory Professional Development can be perceived by teachers merely as a points-gathering exercise.

- When a programme is mandatory, teachers are not making an active choice to engage and can therefore attend sessions in body but not in spirit.

- Sanctions for non-attendance are not easy to enforce and are likely to generate a negative response amongst your staff, in turn dampening motivation.

These risks are worth careful consideration if you are thinking about making your programme compulsory. Your aim should be for a workforce motivated to change, and the last thing you want is for your programme to become a stick with which to beat your staff.

■ 3: **DEVELOPING A COMMUNICATION STRATEGY**

Some schools have no effective communication strategy designed to define the culture of the institution. A school can be rated 'Outstanding' in terms of its student outcomes, but that doesn't necessarily mean it has an outstanding communication strategy in a business sense. In fact, some leaders make the mistake of assuming that once they announce a change, people will adjust and be ready to get started with the new development. This is often the worst way to introduce change and will likely be met with instant resistance. Here are some ways to avoid that outcome:

1. Announce the strategy effectively

Do not make a general announcement about introducing a new strategy; introduce *the* strategy. Your staff need to know about more than just the change that is about to occur. They need to know how that change will affect them as well as *how they will adapt to the change*.

2. Keep everyone informed

Facts versus feelings

If you have a planning team, make sure they know how the change will affect staff. If you ignore this, the planning team is likely to make decisions based on resources such as time and money rather than on feelings and intuitions. This overlooks how people feel, reason and work. While focusing on critical thinking and objective analysis, it is important to understand that taking the feelings of the employees into account is a great way to overcome the barriers that usually hinder organisational changes.

3. Understand the prevailing mentality of your institution

Change is always difficult for organisations that lack an idea of their current state. Trying to introduce and implement change without understanding the prevailing mindset within your school is a common mistake.

Many leaders do not realise that the failure to analyse the current state or feeling in their school will cause a barrier to the change they hope to introduce and implement. The only way to overcome this is to fully understand your school and the attitudes of your workforce before attempting to introduce or suggest any change.

Once you have a full and thorough understanding of your staff mindset, it will become easier to plan and transition to a future state.

Once you understand and manage any obstacles to change management, it will be easy to implement the change. In the end, everyone in your institution will feel comfortable about embracing your programme if you are able to show that you understand the nature of the current state you are about to affect.

4. Use the right language

Language is everything. The language you use sets a tone, and much of the language around improving teaching, or indeed teachers, is loaded with connotations depending on where you are in the world. Ask yourself:

- Are you launching a programme of *Professional Development* or *Professional Learning*?
- Is it *Professional Development* or *Continuing Professional Development*?
- Will your programme have elements of *coaching* or *mentoring*?
- Will people work in *learning groups* or *triads* or be in *coaching pairs* or *partnerships*?
- Will you run *staff training* or *InSET sessions*?

All of these are essentially different ways of saying the same thing, but each communicates a different tone. That tone will dictate the response from your staff.

For example, in the UK, many schools have dropped 'continuing' from 'professional development' or 'professional learning', because it has been said that it should be a given that teachers continue to update their skills, like any other profession. The mere fact that it had to be said added a sense that it was something teachers had to be forced to do, something 'bolted on' to tick a box. Some UK schools now prefer the term 'professional learning' over 'development' as they feel it adds more of an academic feel to the process, whilst others use 'collaborative learning' or 'collaborative development'.

Once you have understood the prevailing mentality of your institution, you should be able to understand what tone to adopt to maximise engagement and motivate your teachers.

Choose your language from the start

Whatever language you choose to use, you should be certain of it from the outset and be clear about what you want to communicate. If collaboration is at the heart of your initiative then tailor your language to

Creating a culture

suit. If you are moving towards a research-based academic approach, then make your language fit that culture. The language used will create a culture from the outset, which brings us back to the overarching principle that your initiative must be fully thought through before you begin.

Make sure your language is consistent

If you alter your language as you go you may be communicating a lack of clarity. You might even give the impression that you are making things up as you go along.

In order to make sure the language you use has a consistent basis, go back to your school policies.

- Do you have a learning and teaching policy or even a policy concerned with staff training?
- What do you already say?
- What are you already communicating?

It is important that your policies align with each other and that there is no contradiction.

Valuing language

You must be mindful of the importance of language. Too many institutions do not understand the impact of language and what is communicated consciously and unconsciously. Your English and humanities department will see things in your writing that your science department may not. Be mindful of your own beliefs around the importance of language. Are you more aligned to the scientists than the linguists? Understanding language and the way you use it should lie at the heart of your communication strategy.

■ 4: GAUGING IMPACT

In order to ensure that your programme is an ongoing success, it is important that you know how to gauge impact. You must be clear about how you are going to gather and collate evidence. This is not only important from your own perspective, in order to understand where your programme is succeeding and where it needs further work, but also in order to convince others of its validity. In order to understand impact you will need to navigate the challenges of cost, and of competition from other internal sources over grade score achievements or other improvements that you wish to prove are products of your Professional Development programme.

1. Impact and cost

When considering the many models available for Professional Development, it is worth remembering that, regardless of the type of school, they are all, to varying degrees, financially led.

Whether your spend relates directly to the model you select or the time needed to release your teachers to engage with your model, cost is a key factor. You may have an executive body in your institution that insists on evidence to support investment in your programme. If you lay out your plans for gauging impact in your initial proposal, all involved should gain from the knowledge that their commitment to improve is impacting on student outcomes.

Facing budget challenges

In 2017, the Teacher Development Trust surveyed a number of UK schools and found that over 20,000 teachers were working in schools where there was no budget for continuing Professional Development at all. Across the entire UK education sector, schools spend an average of just 0.7% of their income on developing their teaching workforce, which equates to just £33 per pupil each year.[4] Even if you find yourself in a system with huge reserves of cash, you will find that what you deliver has to be cost-effective and/or indeed demonstrate a real impact on outcomes; this is a difficult and contentious issue. Measuring the impact of Professional Development within your school needs to be thought through from the outset.

2. Impact and competition

One barrier you might encounter in measuring the success of your initiative is that other leaders may want to claim any improvement in school outcomes for themselves. Their arguments may be valid. Part of the complexity of gauging impact will be tracing impact on outcomes directly back to your programme.

The evidence might seem clear: student outcomes are improving, students are reporting being more engaged in the classroom, and there is a new buzz around teaching and learning that was absent previously. But what, exactly, has led to this cultural change? A re-mapped curriculum? An increased focus on attendance? Newly rewritten schemes of learning? A change in assessment procedures? Or your Professional Development initiative?

---

4   http://tdtrust.org/press-release-21000-teachers-schools-reporting-no-cpd-budget-says-teacher-development-trust-study.

The truth is that all quality, well-considered initiatives should have an impact on outcomes, but research shows that quality Professional Development – a culture of professional learning – will impact on outcomes to a greater level than any other. Think about how you can prove this, as you will need to be able to do so in order to communicate the importance of your programme. Methods to achieve this will be covered in detail in **Chapter Four:** *Measuring Success.*

3. Impact and success

Goals and targets

Ultimately, considering how you will track and measure progress will make you think through precisely what you want to achieve. It will hold you to account and force you to be clear about your desired outcome. It will focus you on how you are going to map out how you are going to meet your goals.

▪ 5: UNDERSTANDING CORE PRINCIPLES

Do you define core principles for your institution or does your institution define your core principles?

Core principles are ideas, aims and values that guide the philosophy and culture of your school. Many schools will have core principles that have been established and defined, such as enabling children to thrive regardless of background, developing respect for cultural diversity, or promoting curiosity and independent learning and development. The core principles of other schools may be defined by the attitudes and beliefs of the teachers in the school, even if they are not spelt out explicitly.

It is important to identify the corresponding core principles that will define your Professional Development programme. It is a good idea to write down these principles, much as you did with your *mission statement* in **Chapter One**, so that you can refer back to them as your programme develops.

These must be principles that you will not compromise on, and they must be guided by the reality of your institution. For example:

- There is little point in deciding that a core principle will be to 'treat all as equal partners' in your programme, and to dispense with guiding experts, if this is not something you can see through in practice in your context. Your staff may be made up of one-third experienced, expert practitioners and two-thirds young teachers in their first few years of practice (more on utilising experts versus equal partners in coaching can be found in **Chapter Three:** *Professional Development Models*).

- A core principle cannot be 'professional learning for all' if you are only going to create a programme for teaching staff.

- You may be a small school, where group work is difficult and teachers working in pairs may be more applicable.

- You may want to create a programme that would allow all teachers to reach Master's-level qualification if they wished, but this can only be stated if it can really happen. It may be that you would like to build a partnership with a local university, but does your institution have the resources to fund such an ambition? What if 5, 10 or 20 members of staff are so enthused that they want to take you up on your offer, but you cannot afford such funding?

You need to make sure that you have the will, conditions and infrastructure to follow through on your core principles.

Understand the core principles of your school, and ensure that these will align with the core principles that will define your programme, before you begin.

Skipping this step will cause your objectives for your programme to fall out of line with the reality of your school or institution, leading to fundamental problems with implementation. A good way to understand how these inter-relate is to map out a diagram like the one in **Figure 3** on the following page that links core principles and outcome goals to the conditions in your school.

Goals and targets

To put it simply, you cannot establish a set of core principles, either explicitly or through the make-up of your programme, that you then contradict in practice. If you undermine the core principles of your programme, it will only have a negative impact. You will be seen to either be unreliable, poor at planning or naïve, any of which will tarnish your initiative. In order to avoid this outcome, look at the following considerations.

Figure 3: *Sketch out a map linking core principles to outcome goals and school context*

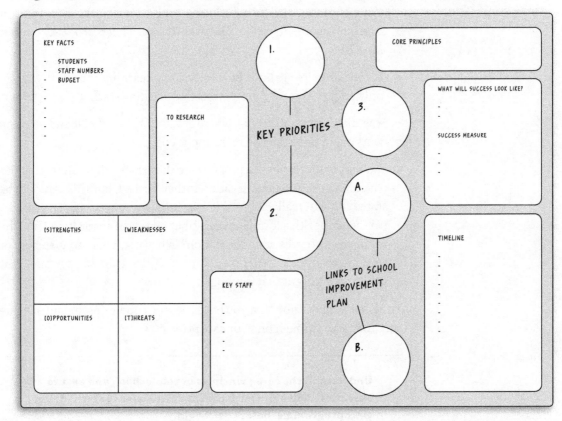

1. Core principles, outcomes and policy

Aligning core principles, core aims and your mission statement

You should establish some key programme outcomes (or *core aims*) from the outset that reflect the core principles you have established as the foundation for your Professional Development programme (you can do this as part of your *mission statement*; see **Chapter One: First Steps**). Your school will already have a series of policies and/or initiatives in place that will need to exist alongside your programme. You must be aware of these to ensure that your core principles and outcome goals do not contradict the requirements of:

- your school's learning and teaching policy relating to lesson planning and delivery
- your school's assessment policy; this may well come down to classroom level and talk about principles around questioning, assessment for learning and group work

Link to existing policies

- your school's appraisal policy/system, which may be linked to teacher performance.

Make sure you are aware of these, and any other pre-existing policies or initiatives that may impact your programme.

2. Policy and risk

Any new initiative that pursues change will challenge the status quo and, as such, invite a certain level of risk. Your initiative will have the overriding objective to improve learning and teaching and therefore outcomes, but it is important to be aware that this may be a mid- to long-term aim requiring teachers to take risks along the way.

Risk and reward

When the Zambian Ministry of Education implemented *Lesson Study* to improve teaching and learning, they were clear that theirs was a ten-year plan. Not only did they invest **time** but they invested a large proportion of their entire **education budget** too. Whereas in Chicago their schools' recent engagement with Professional Development, again through *Lesson Study*, brought about a huge cultural change they didn't expect or necessarily know they needed. They found that for too long they had focused on improving **teachers** rather than **teacher practice**. Whilst this may sound like semantics, it isn't. The historical focus on improving teachers always lay the blame for problems in education at the feet of teachers. By seeking to find ways to improve **teacher practice**, led by teachers themselves, they created a shift in focus more powerful than anyone could have imagined.[5]

These risks may move teachers away from a method of working that has 'proven' outcomes in terms of student results. Asking teachers to change their practice, to try new things and risk their 'successful'

---

5   For further information, see https://www.jica.go.jp/project/zambia/006/outline/index.html and https://www.jica.go.jp/project/zambia/009/materials/ku57pq00002ahn4k-att/Brochure_Lesson_Study_in_Zambia_e.pdf).

outcomes, and therefore risk a successful appraisal, will likely push them out of their comfort zone and push them to try new things. Consider the following question:

In terms of current school policy, what do you do when faced with a teacher who wants to try something new that goes against school policy?

This may not be as radical or concerning as it sounds. It may be that you have a policy whereby students sit in mixed-gender groups or same-sex groups for example. Consider:

- Do you have the authority to override policy for the sake of innovation?
- Would you make this clear from the outset?
- Are you prepared to head off any questions or concerns that others may raise?

Common sense would suggest that any initiative that will improve teaching and learning is a force for good, but you need to be mindful of not offending others. You need to convince others that your initiative is going to impact positively on whole-school outcomes. You also need to remember that whilst you may be convinced of this, so would someone charged with launching any new initiative. Establish from the outset whether you have the power to change policy, or at least influence policy, or if you are to be guided and held by policy.

■ 6: SCALE

Think about the size of your initiative. Are you looking for small improvements or a radical overhaul? Understanding this will help you to understand what you expect in terms of timeframe, which Professional Development models you will use and participation.

1. Timeframe

Is your Professional Development programme a long-term initiative seeking improvement over five or ten years or a one-year quick fix? A lack of understanding about the scale of what you want to achieve will make it hard to make the right decisions and will create a barrier to effective change and the success of your programme.

2. Models

Combining development models

The scale of your programme will impact on your decision-making around Professional Development models, which ones you adopt, and how many. **Chapter Three:** *Professional Development Models* outlines a number of models employed within schools. The majority of schools tune into one form of Professional Development, be it taught sessions, coaching or lesson study. However, a combination of two models can deliver results – for example, putting coaching groups in place to trial and apply new skills learned during taught sessions.

Few schools are able to afford the time or finances to offer *all* models of Professional Development simultaneously, and even if they were, too many options can have a negative effect. Teachers may get lost in the process of picking and choosing and not actually settle into a programme that will have real impact.

As mentioned earlier in this chapter, real impact will come if you truly know your institution and its needs. You must then design a programme to meet the needs identified, selecting and adapting from the models described in the next chapter.

3. Participation

In terms of participation, the 'who' and 'why' must come first, and the 'when' and the 'how' will follow. The **Introduction** touched on the fact that research suggests that the most effective models of Professional Development involve the entire workforce within an institution – this may mean as participants, as experts, in the delivery or in the approval or review. Regardless, you must be clear about who you expect to participate, how and why.

> **Some Professional Development programmes are created entirely to improve those perceived to be *in most need of improving* which, as you can imagine, can be a little daunting and single out certain people to involved in 'the programme'. Likewise other programmes are devised for those capable of *moving to outstanding* which, whilst meant to be more positive, can be just as daunting and/or divisive.**

It can be argued that all teachers, regardless of ability or time in the classroom, can improve their practice.

Considering support staff

Another key question is whether your programme is only for teachers or whether you are catering for support staff. To see that the route to improving teaching is only through teachers sends a negative message to support staff and could affect motivation and morale within your school. Any negativity can filter out and affect your workforce. Avoid giving the impression that the role of support staff is not valued.

It may be outside of your skills remit, or indeed your actual remit, to devise a programme for all, but it may be within your remit to begin that discussion.

Senior teachers and leaders should recognise the need to reflect on their practice in order to improve. Plans to foster improvement should run top-down. If your senior leaders still teach, they should also strive to improve their teaching and/or play a role in improving teaching and learning.

Non-teaching leaders may need a leadership improvement programme to follow or may be the perfect people to write such a programme. Either way, you need to decide to what extent you are going to live by the idea of *holistic involvement*. Do not lose sight of the fact that you impact on the culture of your institution as much by what you don't do as what you do.

•

This chapter has focused on showing you how to establish what you need to think about in order to overcome the barriers to your ideas for change, and to avoid the pitfalls that occur through a lack of adequate planning.

You have established that your programme will need a set of core principles and thought about the scale on which it will need to operate. You have thought about how to go about communicating your programme effectively to a workforce whose motivations you have taken the time to understand. Now that you are clear about what you are aiming to achieve, and understand the context in which you will need to achieve it, you can begin to look at the actual Professional Development model, or models, that you wish to pursue.

Chapter Two summary

This chapter has introduced six basic steps to preparing for implementation of your Professional Development programme.

1. **Understanding external providers**
   - Time, cost, access
   - Not all teachers are the same
   - Moving beyond 'one-size-fits-all'

2. **Improving teacher motivation**
   - How is your programme likely to be perceived?
   - Does your programme offer the right support?
   - Will your programme be mandatory?

3. **Developing a communication strategy**
   - Announce the strategy effectively
   - Keep everyone informed
   - Understand the prevailing mentality of your institution
   - Use the right language

4. **Gauging impact**
   - How much will you assign to professional development?
   - Are you aware of hidden costs?
   - Have you spoken to staff and leaders?

5. **Understanding core principles**
   - Why think about core principles?
   - Core principles and policy
   - Policy and risk

6. **Scale**
   - Timeframe
   - Professional Development models
   - Participation

3   **Professional Development models**

···

In this section we will explore three primary Professional Development models available to you when designing your own programme: coaching, taught Professional Development and lesson study. Each will offer different benefits to your institution and you can even combine the best elements of each to create a model specific to your own needs.

···

INTRODUCTION

Having established the foundations for building your Professional Development programme, it is now time to look at the details of the programme itself. Everything you have thought about so far – your *mission statement*, *core principles* and *core aims/outcomes*, the reality of your school or institution 'on the ground', the mindset of your teachers, and the budget and resources available to you, will inform the choices you are about to make. Bear all of this in mind as you look at the following models, and think about what will work best for you and your particular institution.

The options available to you fall broadly into the following categories, each of which will be looked at in detail:

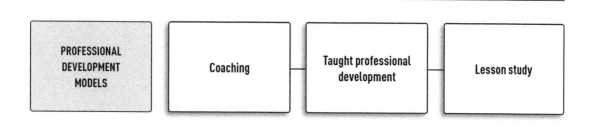

■ 1: **COACHING**

One of the most popular models of professional learning is in-house coaching. In-house coaching uses *group conversation* and *lesson observation* to deliver results and is a flexible form of development training responsive to the speficic environment in your school. The following five steps will take you through the basic coaching programme structure.

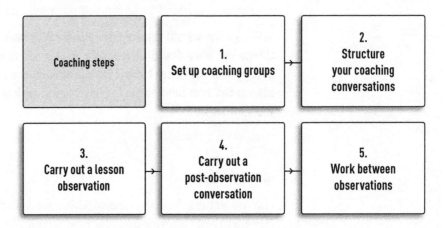

STEP 1: SET UP COACHING GROUPS

First, determine how many people you will have in each of your coaching groups. In-house coaching can work in pairs or larger groups, but groups of three (triads) tend to be the usual model; a different dynamic exists within groups of three in terms of power, which is important when decisions need to be made or an impasse is reached.

Next, decide whether you will be involving all of your staff; this may affect your next decision – whether to pursue equal-status or expert-led triads, or to allow your staff to make that decision for themselves.

Coaching groups: Do you need an expert?

When setting up groups, one of your main considerations will be whether they are to be made up of equally strong teachers or whether one is identified as an *expert*. Some people believe there needs to be an expert to provide ideas and guidance, tackle common misconceptions and direct people towards accepted good practice. Others feel that more powerful change can be driven by the equal status of those involved as it frees them from the fear of judgement.

Equal-status triads: If you are pursuing a model of equal status within your triads to avoid fear of judgement, think about how you will place middle-tier and senior leaders, newly qualified teachers and senior teachers. To some extent, the size and make-up of your institution is a factor here and may dictate your *core principles* in relation to teacher heirarchy and your programme (see **Chapter 2** for more on core principles).

Expert-led triads: It may be that you want to take advantage of your school structure and assign a senior member of staff to each triad so as to ensure they are outcomes-driven. An alternative approach to the expert-led triad is to place a 'knowledgeable other' within each triad: a senior teacher in terms of ability but not in terms of management structure.

Staff-driven triads: You may decide to allow staff to pick their own pairs or triads. This can be hugely empowering but it can also encourage *safe selection*, with people staying firmly within their comfort zone and choosing to work only with their trusted colleagues or friends.

Be alert to 'safe selection'

Whichever model you decide upon, remember once again to think your programme through fully in the context of the needs and reality of your institution.

STEP 2: STRUCTURE YOUR COACHING CONVERSATIONS

The coaching model relies on structuring effective coaching conversations before and after lesson observations. There is obvious value in giving staff a chance to talk about your Professional Development programme at leisure, but a conversation without structure is one best saved for the staff room. The conversations that take place in your triads (or pairs/groups) must be given clear direction. Otherwise, in a worst-case scenario, you might find that your coaching pairs or triads descend into unnecessary or counter-productive chat or gossip.

Structuring to limit gossip

Many models to structure conversations exist and should be provided in order to keep the discussion anchored to its *core purpose*. Such models focus those involved and drive actual outcomes by ensuring that conversations remain tied to learning and teaching in the classroom. Pre-made pro formas outlining the model you wish to use should be issued to your coaching pairs or triads. With a pro forma to begin the process, your staff will be aware that coaching conversations are not an opportunity to chat.

Areas of focus for groups: ☑

- [ ] QUALITY OF INSTRUCTION
- [ ] PACE
- [ ] STUDENTS' ACTIVE PARTICIPATION
- [ ] HIERARCHICAL QUESTIONING
- [ ] QUESTIONING ACROSS THE CLASS BETWEEN STUDENTS
- [ ] TAKE UP TIME GIVEN
- [ ] THINK-PAIR-SHARE
- [ ] PAIR WORK
- [ ] GROUP WORK
- [ ] PEER ASSESSMENT
- [ ] EFFECTIVE LESSON DESIGN
- [ ] EFFECTIVELY PITCHED LESSON SUITED TO THE CLASS
- [ ] DATA USED TO INFORM LESSON DESIGN
- [ ] EFFECTIVE MODELLING OF TASK
- [ ] DIFFERENTIATION TO SUPPORT 'SEND' STUDENTS
- [ ] MATERIALS TO SUPPORT 'EAL' STUDENTS
- [ ] LESSON CLEARLY SEQUENCED

The power of shared ideas

Remember, you are asking staff to challenge each other to improve. You may want to put in place training around the coaching conversation and how to handle potential difficulties that this might cause. For example, not all teachers are able to recognise their strengths. Likewise, some teachers have an inaccurate picture of their abilities, which can be extremely difficult to deal with. How do you work to improve someone who feels they have no need to improve? These are questions you should have already considered more generally in **Chapter Two:** *Breaking Down Barriers*, but now you should revisit those questions in the context of your chosen Professional Development model.

The sample model in **Figure 4** structures your coaching conversations around seven key concepts: *Strengths, Targets, Ideas, Reality; Try, Evaluate, Apply.*

Figure 4: *S.T.I.R T.E.A (a coaching conversation structure)*

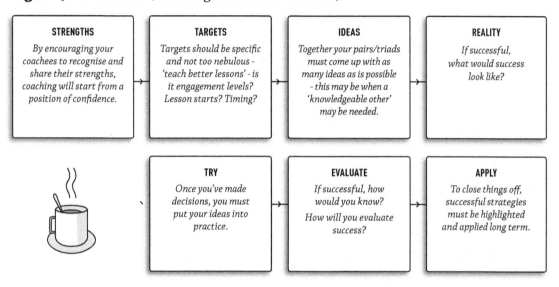

STRENGTHS

By encouraging your coachees to recognise and share their strengths, coaching will start from a position of confidence.

TARGETS

Targets should be specific and not too nebulous - 'teach better lessons' - is it engagement levels? Lesson starts? Timing?

IDEAS

Together your pairs/triads must come up with as many ideas as is possible - this may be when a 'knowledgeable other' may be needed.

REALITY

If successful, what would success look like?

TRY

Once you've made decisions, you must put your ideas into practice.

EVALUATE

If successful, how would you know? How will you evaluate success?

APPLY

To close things off, successful strategies must be highlighted and applied long term.

COACHING MODELS *(A brief overview)*

The STIR TEA coaching model above is an approach devised to support the thinking described in this book, and it builds on established and recognised models for structuring coaching conversations. The most common of these are GROW and STRIDE:

G.R.O.W

The Grow model has been one of the most widely-used coaching models since it was first conceived by Sir John Whitmore in the 1980s and is described in detail in his book *Coaching for Performance* (Nicholas Brealey, 1992). It is deceptively simple and its steps lie at the core of many coaching conversation models.

>

Goal	What do you want to achieve? What is your desired *goal* or outcome?
Reality	Where are you now? What is the *reality* of your current situation and what obstacles do you face?
Options	What steps can you take next? What *options* are available to you that might help you to achieve your desired goal?
Will	What steps will you actually take? What *will* you do?

S.T.R.I.D.E

The STRIDE model for coaching conversations was devised by Will Thomas and Alastair Smith, authors of *Coaching Solutions: Practical Ways to Improve Performance in Education* (Thomas and Smith, 2004), and is another process-based framework to help structure a coaching conversation. With its emphasis on positivity, it encourages coachee empowerment:

Strengths	What are the strengths of the coachee?
Target	What is the desired outcome of your coaching conversation(s)?
Reality	What is your current situation and what obstacles lie in your way?
Ideas	How might you tackle these challenges?
Decide	Decide upon an approach.
Evaluate	Track and measure your progress.

The STIR TEA model expands on these frameworks and retains the emphasis on both *positivity* and *outcomes*. These outcome-based approaches are forward-thinking and will encourage progress. A coachee focus is important in helping to maintain self-esteem at high levels – the skill is in picking up an individual's strengths and feeding them back throughout the coaching process.

The true purpose behind the coaching conversation is *to facilitate change that is owned by those involved*. The questions asked, and the manner in which those questions are asked, is paramount as it is here that solutions and ideas for improvement are generated. Effective coaching conversations should be challenging but supportive. If this is the case then people will feel free to share ideas.

When people are given the space to share ideas and find solutions to their own problems, it strengthens confidence and brings about sustained change.

Thinking about time

Coaching has a proven track record, but of the range of Professional Learning initiatives available to you it does make significant demands on staff time.

Time will always be an issue for teaching staff (it was one of the barriers to change identified in **Chapter Two:** *Breaking Down Barriers*). In an ideal scenario, you would create such a deep culture of improvement that your staff work to find the time for themselves, but this ambition rarely matches reality. The coaching model has two time-consuming dimensions: **coaching conversations** and **lesson observations**. Lesson observations in particular present a drain on time as they involve teachers sitting in on whole classes. The most effective way to manage these activities is to **timetable** them.

Timetabling will require forethought and forward planning, but will ensure that you minimise disruption to your teachers and their busy teaching schedules. Ask yourself:

- *Are your coaching pairs or triads from within the same faculty or department?*

  Intra-faculty work makes sense in principle, but most schools tend to timetable classes within faculties at the same time. This can make sitting in on each other's classrooms problematic. Another danger of intra-faculty work is that conversations can turn into a dialogue about sharing ideas or resources, or maybe even just general chat about the faculty in general. This might make people feel better but it won't bring about long-term sustainable change. Coaching to *improve teaching* needs to go beyond this to maximise the impact of the time you dedicate to it.

- *How will timetabling coaching affect your budget?*

  Giving time on a timetable impacts staffing levels and therefore money. Extra time means extra money, and if you are answering to a finance director they will likely need both a pedagogical and financial rationale for this.

Coaching requires a significant time investment from the outset. Not finding time for your staff to engage with your initiative risks no buy-in, or poor results from those staff that do engage. You do not want create a belief that your new initiative is just 'one more thing' to find time for.

Key questions for a coaching conversation:

1. WHAT IS YOUR BIGGEST SUCCESS OVER THE LAST YEAR?

2. HOW DID YOU BRING ABOUT THAT SUCCESS?

3. WHAT WOULD SUCCESS LOOK LIKE IN THE REAL WORLD?

4. WHAT OUTCOMES ARE YOU LOOKING FOR NOW AND IN THE LONG TERM?

5. WHAT HAVE YOU TRIED RECENTLY?

6. HOW WILL YOU BE ABLE TO MEASURE SUCCESS?

Choose your language

The language used in coaching conversations is key. You need to be non-judgemental and non-confrontational, but beyond that you need to be in tune with your coachee. For example:

- Will you talk of 'we' or 'you'?
- Will you talk in terms of the *head*, asking what participants what they 'think', or will you talk in terms of *heart*, asking what they 'feel' about a situation?

Coaches need to be able to think on their feet. When resistance is felt, the coach needs to decide whether to push or hold back and wait for a better moment. In such circumstances you can always rely on asking what the implications or consequences are of not changing. Well-considered, expert questions move those involved beyond superficial, surface change and will bring about long-term improvement. Better still, if success is seen to come about through greater dialogue and collaboration, you will begin to see change in the *culture* within your institution.

STEP 3: CARRY OUT A LESSON OBSERVATION

Lesson observations can be perceived in different ways. For a lot of teachers they are a tool with which to measure the quality of their teaching and, therefore, their ability to teach. To some teachers they are a means by which they can show off and develop their skills. But there will also be those who greet the idea of observation with fear and apprehension. With the quality of teaching forming the basis of many school's appraisal systems, which in turn is invariably linked to pay progression, observations are a loaded entity.

Whilst there is a great deal of current research around the effectiveness of lesson observations to judge the quality of teaching in the classroom, peer observation as a means to improve practice is invaluable. Non-judgemental peer observations should be more natural, allowing the teacher under observation to be more relaxed. Such observations should also be focused on a specific element of practice, usually agreed beforehand in a coaching conversation, rather than attempting to provide a holistic overview of everything. The observation takes place to improve practice; it is not about judgement.

Peer observation

The importance of targeted observation

Being able to observe a teacher teach in any subject area and identify precisely how they can improve their outcomes is a skill that develops over many years. It is therefore important to stress to those involved in coaching that this is not what is demanded. Through discussion around strengths and areas to develop following one of the *model coaching structures* described earlier, a specific focus for observation should be agreed. You may even want to ask your coaching pairs or triads to create their own observation pro forma or set of questions. By doing this,

Focusing on specifics

- all involved are very clear about the focus of the observation;
- it is clear that no holistic judgement is being made, and
- by focusing on one aspect of teacher practice, there is a greater likelihood of progress/change being made.

Avoid falling into the trap of wanting to see 'outstanding' improvement without having a clear idea of what this means. To achieve this, huge changes across a range of areas need to be made over a period of time. Trying to change everything at once is not practical. It is like trying to tell a footballer to score more goals, or a golfer to reduce their handicap to single figures. Improvement needs to be attached to specific targets, allowing your teachers to improve one part of their practice at a time. Aside from being unrealistic in practice, if wide-ranging simultaneous change is attempted, it then becomes difficult to isolate precisely what has changed when you come to evaluate the outcomes of your programme (see **Chapter 4**: *Measuring Success*). If it

Achieving incremental improvement

is difficult to measure and evaluate, it is also difficult to replicate, and importantly to celebrate, the results.

To what extent should you involve students in observations?

Every day your students are engaged in hours of lessons. Students are exposed to a variety of subjects, delivered in a variety of ways by a variety of teachers. More than anyone else in your institution, your students know what is good and what is bad, what works and what does not. As such, most student bodies are an **untapped resource**.

Whilst you must be mindful of the fact that some teachers might be sceptical about involving students in observations, your student body *must* be involved in your initiative. At the very least, you have a duty to inform them that you are embarking on a new programme to make learning and teaching even better. This message can come from individual teachers or from your leadership team.

Some schools actively involve students in the entire process. Some have trained both teachers and students as coaches and their triads are made up of teachers and students. Since the observations have no element of judgement, all involved are free to make suggestions and consider questions around pedagogical methods employed in the classroom. Whilst you might encounter a certain amount of reticence around the idea of involving students, done well this approach can bring about a huge cultural change.

Learning and teaching happens in schools for the good of the students and yet too often school can feel like something that is 'done' to them. Imagine the possibilities if you engage students in dialogue around what their teachers do well, what they do less well and what and how they could improve their practice. Consider the culture change that could be brought about by such an honest and open environment where discussions about the process of learning and teaching prevail.

As we move away from simply teaching knowledge, and increasingly towards teaching skills such as teamwork and problem solving, open dialogue between all school stakeholders has the potential to offer so much; it is a case of redefining who the stakeholders really are in schools. Some schools may not like the idea of involving students in improving teacher practice out of fear of offending teachers. But where does this place students? What message does it send to them? School is all about student learning, and their engagement in the development of those teaching them is invaluable.

Effective coaching comes about through regular conversations between those involved and regular short, non-invasive observations. Each person involved in your coaching pairs or triads should know the others' strengths and areas to develop intimately so that everyone is working for the good of the others.

Observation checklist: ☑

- ☐ IS THE TEACHER WORKING TOO HARD?
- ☐ IS THE LEARNING PITCHED AT THE RIGHT LEVEL FOR THE STUDENTS IN THE CLASS?
- ☐ IS THERE CHALLENGE IN THE LESSON DESIGN?
- ☐ DO THE STUDENTS FEEL ENTHUSED?
- ☐ ARE THE TASKS BROKEN DOWN?
- ☐ ARE THERE REGULAR OPPORTUNITIES TO GAUGE THE LEARNING TAKING PLACE?
- ☐ IS QUESTIONING EFFECTIVE?
- ☐ ARE STUDENTS WORKING EFFECTIVELY IN GROUPS OR JUST SAT IN GROUPS?
- ☐ ARE STUDENTS ENCOURAGED TO SOLVE PROBLEMS OR ARE THEY BEING TOLD ANSWERS?

So far, your pairs or triads have met to discuss areas of strength and areas that each person wants to improve, and have carried out an initial observation. Now, it is time to reflect on the findings of that observation.

STEP 4: CARRY OUT A POST-OBSERVATION CONVERSATION

The key outcome of the post-observation discussion is to use the findings from the observation to devise the next step: to research an identified aspect of teacher practice, and to begin to alter and adapt that practice in the classroom. The conversation following the first observation is incredibly important: it cements the relationship of trust between those involved and it is where the most significant amount of learning should take place.

It is here that those involved will begin to see the value in effective coaching and should now understand how they might be able to improve. Balance is key to the post-observation conversation. The conversations between coach and coachee need to be supportive in order to encourage the coachee to put forward their analysis and ideas from the observation session:

Developing trust

- the coach needs to ensure that the coachee receives enough praise and reinforcement to feel confident, while making sure that this praise is genuine;
- the coach needs to ask enough questions to tease out of the coachee what needs to happen next without frustrating them with a lack of specific guidance; and equally
- the coach needs to make sure that when they provide advice and guidance to move things forward, they do not disempower the coachee.

Learning to listen

Listening skills need to be at a maximum – deep listening without any interruption. The objective of the post-observation conversation is to reveal what is not working as well as it could and, therefore, to suggest what should be happening differently. It may be a lack of confidence or understanding of a concept that this conversation should be revealing. If the flow of the conversation is interrupted or taken in another direction, the opportunity to identify an area of change may be lost.

Post-observation in-school education and training

After lesson observations, you might want to consider providing in-house Professional Development sessions, traditionally known as InSET (In-school Education and Training). These sessions could be taught sessions based around key identified topics, such as *creating pace* or *engaging disconnected boys*. These sessions could be created and delivered by your own teaching staff or you could engage external providers (see the next section on *Taught Professional Development* for more detail on external providers in this context).

A simple trick for conversation

A conversational technique that might help you is to repeat the last phrase spoken in order to move the discussion forward:

Coach: How do you feel your questioning helped the higher learners?

Coachee: On the whole well, but I feel I could have done more.

Coach: Could have done more?

Coachee: ...

While this is just one technique and must not be used to an extent that it appears obvious and contrived, it can be highly effective. Remember that if you are going to offer up such techniques in coaching-based training across the whole of your school, they will not be a secret for long. Make sure that the relationship between coach and coachee is built on *truth* and *collaboration*, and not much will go wrong.

These sessions would supplement the learning gained from lesson observations and coaching conversations. They can either be tailored to the needs of pairs/triads/groups, reactive as their work progresses, or devised beforehand, pre-empting key skills and needs of your institution. There are obvious advantages to reactive, tailor-made Professional Development as it allows for exploration and moves away from a prescriptive approach.

Reactive versus prescriptive training

Done well and created and delivered in-house, teachers will feel empowered and, if your approach allows it, will feel free to select the Professional Development sessions they need.

Empowering teachers

Another approach is for teachers to lead their own post-observation training sessions. This is essentially an extended version of the 'independent research' referenced earlier, but on a larger scale. Teachers

Teacher-led training

would conduct research and create their own solutions and their own approach to improvement, which they would then share as a taught Professional Development session.

STEP 5: WORK BETWEEN OBSERVATIONS

By this stage, coaching pairs or triads should be making much headway. They should have built a strong relationship and helped to identify each other's strengths and target areas, and should have a good idea of what success will look like once achieved. Having car-

Identifying areas of development

ried out a detailed and specific observation, they should now be at the stage of discussing what should happen next. It may be that specific areas of development have been identified or more broad, general concepts. Look at the following example:

- it may be identified that there is a lack of pace in a lesson *(broad)*
- it may be identified that a lack of pace in the start of a lesson leads to low-level disruption in low-ability boys *(specific)*

Whilst a more specific area of focus is preferred and should be found through the pre- and post-observation conversation, either of the examples above would benefit from some reading around *active learning time*, maybe specific to boys. You might want to ask:

- Is there any research around concentration levels, specifically boys?
- Is there an opportunity here for a small-scale research project to be carried out in your school led by one of your coaching pairs or triads?
- How do the boys identified in the observation perform in other lessons, with other teachers?
- Is the outcome of the first observation to get into someone else's lesson to see a different way of starting lessons, or injecting pace?
- If no one has any strategies proven to inject pace into lessons with a high ratio of low-ability boys, is this group suitable to devise such strategies to be shared with all?

Imagine such outcomes from every pair or triad within your school, with multiple small-scale research projects involving your students led by your staff taking place simultaneously. Consider the cultural shift as teachers are empowered to improve teaching within your school. Here, the collaboration between staff and students has the potential to lead to improved outcomes for all, driven by all. Conferences involving the whole school could be carried out once per term, allowing pairs/triads to share their work, their findings and their improvement strategies. If students are involved in the process, they too could share evidence of the improvement of student outcomes through their involvement in the improvement of teacher practice.

Coaching checklist:

- ☐ SIZE UP YOUR INSTITUTION
- ☐ WHO TO INVOLVE
- ☐ PAIRS OR TRIADS
- ☐ EQUAL STATUS
- ☐ USE KNOWLEDGEABLE OTHERS
- ☐ SENIOR STAFF MEMBERS AND HOW TO PLACE THEM
- ☐ STRUCTURED CONVERSATION PRO FORMA
- ☐ DEALING WITH TIME
- ☐ TO GROUP WITHIN DEPARTMENTS OR NOT

The secret to effective coaching

*The beauty of effective coaching is that once pairs/triads are in place, teachers will continue to grow and improve their practice together. But, as with any initiative you implement, it must be effective and collaborative, and it must be a system with quality at its heart. Quality will bring about results, and results will maintain momentum. Essentially, effective coaching will demonstrate to teachers that **they** hold the key to improving teaching.*

■ 2: **TAUGHT PROFESSIONAL DEVELOPMENT**

In contrast to the opportunity for free-flowing exploration offered by coaching, taught in-school training provides a more prescriptive approach to Professional Development. There are benefits to such an approach but, as covered in **Chapter Two**: *Breaking Down Barriers*, it is important to keep sight of what is best for your institution and your staff, and not be seduced by what might be tempting initiatives in themselves but not right for you. Taught Professional Development, whether delivered through external providers or by internal experts, can be scheduled and costed, and works best when tailored to your staff needs.

Tailoring teaching to meet staff needs

Various strands of taught Professional Development can be created for different levels of staff so that all are catered for. These could include:

- new staff or those who have recently joined your institution,
- support or administrative staff
- class teachers
- middle management
- senior management.

Staff can then take a path based on their personal desired outcome, or your institution's desired outcome for them. For example:

1. *New staff* can embark on an **Orientation programme** devised to educate them in your school systems. Your appraisal system can reflect this by linking a successful probation period to the completion of your orientation package. This can work for new support, administrative or teaching staff.

2. Teachers wishing to become *advanced skills teachers* or *specialist subject teachers* may follow a **Teaching and Learning programme**.

3. Staff recently appointed to *middle management* positions, or on a step towards middle management, can embark on an **Educational Leadership programme**.

4. At the *highest aspiration* level, those hoping to become *headteachers* may follow an in-house or national **Qualification for Headship**, (assuming one exists in your district/country). Teachers wishing to take their *advanced skills*, *specialist subject* or *middle management* training to the next level might wish to pursue **Master's-level**

qualifications in Teaching and Learning or Educational Leadership. These can be made up of selected units and/or research paths that can umbrella all of the above scenarios with units or research selected to fit the desired aspiration.

Figure 5: *Tiers of learning: Taught Professional Development programmes*

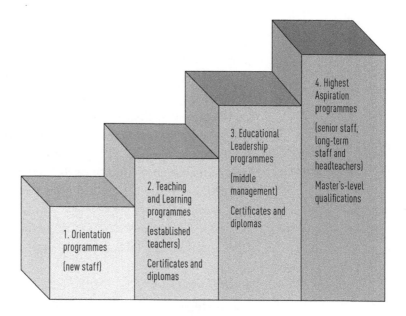

There are many different staff requirements, and your Professional Development programme should ideally cater for all. This will also allow you to support staff throughout their career at your school or institution. Think about this example:

Catering for all

- A recently qualified teacher has just been employed in your school and is highly aspirational. They will require orientation at first, but further down the line they intend to excel as a classroom practitioner, and beyond that go on to experience middle management as a Head of Department in order to one day make the final step to Headteacher. In support of all this, they believe wholeheartedly in research-based practice and are very clear that they want to progress to Master's level.

This teacher will benefit, over the course of their career, from a Professional Development programme model that caters to all stages. Equally, as a new staff member, they will be pleased to find that there are specific Professional Development programmes available to cater for them throughout their career.

If you fear that providing extensive training might result in your staff training themselves up only to move on to another school, as some do, remember the positive message that an ongoing development structure in your school will give to those who wish to engage in it.

Realising ambitions

You can apply this logic to any staff member – your recently hired Head of Department, already some way down their career path, or the Deputy Principal working to take on the Headship in the next five years. The same goes for support staff, administrative staff and teachers, all of whom will be looking to see how your institution can help to realise their ambitions. It is good business practice to develop and build your own staff, and grow your next middle leaders and senior team.

Let us look in more detail at these four tiers of Taught Professional Development, and look at how to implement or update them.

1. Orientation

You are likely to have some sort of orientation process in place at your school already, and if you do, you can use this as a starting point for your new programme. Survey staff that were hired two or three years ago.

- What did they get as their orientation package?
- What were they taught that helped them?
- What did they learn that they did not really need to know?

Updating existing programmes

Institutions can often run orientation packages that are outdated, essentially lagging systems by a few years. If this is the case, not only is this package redundant, but it will also suggest to your new staff that Professional Development is not valued in your institution. Examine what your school currently offers and do so with an honest eye in terms of quality. For example:

- Does your orientation package cater to the specific conditions of your institution? Could you make it more streamlined and targeted?

- Does your package include ongoing orientation support? For example, your orientation plan could require new staff to meet regularly throughout the first year for further training and support.

- What printed material do you supply to support your orientation programme? For example: a list of who to go to for specific requirements; a list of available student services; a binder or booklet outlining school rules, procedures and resources; and, if they exist in written form, a copy of your school's core principles (see **Chapter Two** for more on core principles).

Taking professional development online

- Does your orientation programme have an online dimension? With the availability of adapted takeaways and IT systems that confirm that those signed up for the orientation package have accessed it in full, there is a strong argument to include an online element to your orientation programme.

Your orientation package must work for *your* institution. It should reflect not only the principles and objectives of your school but the challenging day-to-day realities that your new teachers will face and perhaps not necessarily expect.

2 & 3. **Teaching and Learning** and **Educational Leadership**

Having looked at orientation, the next tier of taught programmes includes Teaching and Learning and Educational Leadership. However, you might find it useful to jump forward and look at your highest aspiration qualifications first (see below), and then work backwards – being aware of what your programme will aim for at the highest level might influence your decisions about these middle tiers.

In terms of *teaching and learning* and *educational leadership*, there are many courses available on the market and you may already have objectives – and therefore courses – in mind. For example, you may intend to look into courses that specialise in:

- English as an Additional Language (EAL)
- Special Educational Needs and Disability (SEND)
- Digital learning

Balancing choice

There are many such advanced skills and specialist subject areas but be careful that you do not spread your Professional Development ambitions, or your funding, too thinly. Choice is good, but too much can be overwhelming for staff and also cause participants to become dispersed too widely across numerous small groups. Small groups do not always produce the best outcomes, are rarely cost-effective and, ultimately, may even lead to the cancellation of their course. If too few sign up for a session or series of sessions, that course is unlikely to go ahead.

Using external providers: Parkside Federation Academies

When Parkside Federation Academies (PFA) explored their Professional Development offer, they looked for a solution that would allow them to develop a programme that would be personal to their institution but also deliver an accredited qualification. Cambridge Assessment International Education **Professional Development Qualifications** (PDQs) offered a respected certified qualification that could be tailored to meet the specific needs of the PFA. There are currently four PDQ programmes available:

- Teaching and Learning
- Educational Leadership
- Teaching Bilingual Learners
- Teaching with Digital Technologies

These are designed for practising teachers and aspiring education leaders, or those in leadership roles. The PDQ programmes are written by a programme leader within an institution, in alignment with the framework of Cambridge International. The programmes are quality-assured and approved, providing they are at the required level; Cambridge International train and accredit a programme leader in your centre. The programme leader runs the programme but does not necessarily have to deliver every session.

The Cambridge International PDQ Diploma consists of three learning and assessment modules. Teachers/leaders must complete each module successfully before moving on to the next. The first module can be completed on its own as a certificate, which then provides a strong foundation for progress to Modules 2 and 3 and the Diploma. Each module is assessed through a portfolio of evidence of practice, learning and reflection using templates set by Cambridge International. These portfolios of evidence are submitted when ready for examination and, providing the candidate has met the standard, they are then certified.

For more on the PFA, see **Chapter 5:** *Real-World Example – Parkside Federation Academies, UK.*

Many organisations offer Professional Development programmes in these areas that run over one day or a series of days. Such organisations will come to you, or your staff will go to them. Be warned, navigating options offered by external providers can be a minefield; it can be costly and quality can vary massively. As organisations market their wares, they tend to make grand claims but few, if any, guarantees.

Negotiating with external providers

As before, research is key. It is a buyer's market so enter into discussion about your needs and about price. Try to avoid 'off-the-peg' options that will not allow you to adapt courses to your specific needs (see **Chapter Two:** *Breaking Down Barriers* for more on the benefits, and pitfalls, of using external providers). When choosing your specialist courses, keep these questions in mind:

- Does the course offer genuine quality?
- Will the course have demonstrable impact on outcomes?
- Is it portable, with value to those involved? In other words, is it certificated by a recognised and respected organisation?

The perfect taught Professional Development course delivered by an external provider will be one that is validated and standardised, but also gives you the flexibility to tailor it to the needs of your institution.

4. Highest aspiration qualifications

What will you offer on the highest rung of your Professional Development ladder? At this level, you might be thinking about:

- National Headship professional qualifications. These exist in a number of countries and can be government-accredited.

Going to Master's level

- Master's-level programmes. Many Master's-level programmes exist that allow flexibility in terms of the research element. Those who specialise in Learning and Teaching would pursue a final dissertation in this field. The same can also work for those interested in the field of SEND, Departmental Leadership or subject-specific research. Those aspiring to Headship or even executive or trust-level leadership would tailor their large-scale research project to fit, possibly through secondment to a temporary post.

Master's-level programmes are delivered through universities. Many school trusts are linked to universities and, therefore, would have an obvious partner within their chain of institutions to link to. For those

Access and distance learning

not so fortunate, a number of world-renowned universities have distance-learning programmes, including University College London/ Institute of Education (IoE), who are ranked number one in the world for educational research.

Your highest-aspiration qualification need not be a Master's-level programme, but it is important to consider where staff can aim to get – do not forget the example of a freshly qualified member of staff with a plan to reach the top of your institution.

If you *are* going to go to Master's level, consider funding models working on the most extreme scenario – that dozens of your staff want to sign up in the first year. Can you afford such take-up or do you need to limit numbers? If you are going to limit numbers, how will you go about it?

- Will access to the programme be on a first-come, first-serve basis, or
- Will you use a points-based scheme with factors such as length of service, management points and so on taken into consideration?

Whatever your highest-aspiration qualification or programme, do your research and be guided by quality first and other factors second.

Taught Professional Development and budget

....

Cost is always a consideration when looking at taught Professional Development options. Because such programmes are invariably modular, the financial cost can be spread. Many institutions offering higher-level degrees tend to offer partial funding, with the candidate funding a percentage of the course themselves via *salary sacrifice*. If you are unfamiliar with salary sacrifice, essentially, staff members sign an agreement stating that, should they leave a short time after they have completed a course, they would be liable to pay back the money funded to them. The percentage to be paid back steps down as time goes on – the full amount within a year, 50 percent within two years, and so on. Also, it is often a part of the agreement that the research carried out be proven to impact positively on the school.

Survey your staff or form a working group consisting of a handful of staff across different subject areas and with a range of experience and aspirations (see **Chapter One:** *First Steps* for more on working groups). Use your findings to support your decisions about which courses and offerings are suitable for your staff.

With certificates and diplomas for both Teaching and Learning and Educational Leadership sandwiched in between your orientation programme and your higher aspirational qualifications, you now have an example of a tiered programme that should satisfy your newly qualified teacher as they work towards meeting their long-term goals. Those with less lofty ambitions can select where and when to become involved and those part way down their career path can enter at the appropriate level.

■ 3: LESSON STUDY

Lesson study is a Japanese model for improving teaching through research led by teachers. The name for lesson study in Japanese is *Jugyokenkyu* – *jugyo* translating as 'teaching' and *kenkyu* translating as 'research'. One way to think about this is as a more sophisticated form of coaching. The similarities are that teachers work in small groups and, through research, seek to solve an issue and improve teaching. The differences are that the group work together to plan a model lesson having conducted extensive research. There is also much greater emphasis on an outside expert – a knowledgeable 'other' – to aid the process.

Using 'knowledgeable others'

As with coaching, teachers carry out a lesson observation, but unlike coaching, many people observe at once. In Japan it is seen as an honour to carry out a lesson for lesson study, and many are invited. Sometimes, there can be more observers in the room than students. The problem the study seeks to resolve, or the issue it seeks to improve, is usually very specific. It is never a case of just *improving the teaching of English or Maths*, or even *improving the teaching and writing of fractions*. Part of the strength of lesson study lies in its narrow focus: a lesson might look at *improving the teaching of constructing complex sentence forms* or *teaching adding fractions to Year 6*.

How does lesson study work?

Look at **Figure 6** to see the cycle of steps required to carry out lesson study:

Figure 6: *The lesson study cycle*

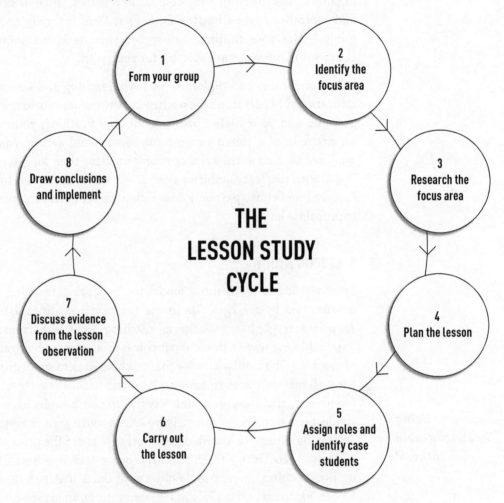

Let us look at each of these steps in a little more detail:

1. **Form your group.** Choose a 'knowledgeable other', or expert, who can access up-to-date research to form part of your group.

2. **Identify the focus area.** Narrow the focus to a specific question or concept.

3. **Research the focus area.** With the help of your chosen expert, ask the group to gather all information they can around the focus area.

4. **Plan the lesson.** Instruct the group to come together and plan, in intricate detail, a lesson that they believe will address the issue and improve the teaching of the chosen area of focus.

   If done well, the level of detail for this lesson will be unlike anything most teachers are used to. The group should seek to eradicate any unseen potential issues, address any questions that students might ask and address any possible direction that students may take the lesson in.

5. **Assign roles and identify case students.** Choose one of the teachers in your group to teach the lesson.

   Identify key roles within the group. Identify case students and assign teachers to focus students or focus areas. There may be a number of areas that you want to look at, for example:

   - questioning
   - responses to questions
   - engagement levels
   - group work
   - peer assessment.

   You might want to invite teachers from other schools. Such public research lessons can then become reciprocal across districts or regions.

6. **Carry out the lesson.** The group should now observe the taught lesson. It is important to understand the distinction that *the teaching of the lesson is being observed, and not the teacher.* The purpose of the observation is to dissect and test the lesson design. Essentially, this is your way of reflecting on the quality of the research that your group, with the help of your designated expert, has explored.

   Observing teaching, not the teacher

   It is worth repeating that those observing are not judging the quality of the delivery of the class by the teacher, but rather the teaching of that particular lesson. In other words, the emphasis is on the lesson itself, the way it is structured and the way that it plays out.

   Review your policies

   Notes can be taken, film can be shot and students should be interviewed after the observation. Bear in mind you will need to adhere to your policy regarding student involvement in research at this point.

7. **Discuss evidence from the lesson observation.** The observation has served as a means to gather a wealth of evidence; the next

stage is to review that evidence. Ask the group to collate and share their findings. All those involved in the observation should formally meet to present what they have found – their *observations* – and a detailed discussion should take place.

8. **Draw conclusions and implement.** Ask the group to draw conclusions about the success of the endeavour. Has the group found a more effective way to teach writing complex sentences, to add fractions, or whatever it was they set out to do? This sizeable piece of work should then be shared and go on to impact on the particular aspect of teaching across school, district or region.

In terms of how to set up lesson study in your institution, many of the considerations that must be dealt with are similar to those covered in the discussions around coaching and taught professional development:

• Who will you involve?

• Will you impose groups or give freedom of choice?

• How will you give people time to be free to engage with the initiative?

• How will you engage 'knowledgeable others'? Will you look to a local or linked university, or to staff currently at your institution who have a suitable knowledge base?

• How will you prepare your participants? A large-scale lesson study session is very different to a standard observation and your teachers will need to be prepared to adapt their expectations.

Thinking about scale

You might also want to think about how wide you would like to cast your net. Are you looking to involve other schools in Lesson Study? Whilst this is the norm in Japan and has become the norm in certain districts in the USA, it is less common elsewhere and it may be that you want to keep lesson study in-house.

In Japan, lesson study is intrinsic to the professional culture of teaching and has played a major part in curriculum reform over the last few decades. It has been a part of school, district and government-wide strategy for improving pupil learning, putting student-centred learning at the heart of teaching, for two hundred years. It offers the opportunity to change the culture within schools, but this does not happen overnight. Lesson study delivers benefits over a period of time and requires commitment on the part of your institution and your staff.

Lesson Study: What works well

The following advice has been compiled from lesson study initiatives around the world and will guide your thinking if you are choosing to implement lesson study in your school.

Select a manageable size group of teachers – three works well – who are likely to enjoy the challenge and the process of lesson study. Remember you are looking to get initial buy-in by selling the virtues of lesson study so picking the right people to pilot your initiative is vital.

Make it clear from the start that it is a non-judgemental process. Many schools believe Lesson Study works well when there is at least one member of the senior team involved and it is paramount that you have a mix of teaching experience as well as access to a knowledgeable friend, even if that friend is a library or internet resource.

Hold a meeting with them to set out expectations and ground rules. **In a Lesson Study all members of the group are of equal status**. Ask the group to agree some parameters which are based on identified school, class or subject/year group needs. Decide on parameters you are going to set. For example, are you going to insist teachers use common forms for lesson planning, observation or analysis? How much time are you going to give teachers in terms of time? If you can't give extra time, can you protect their time on certain days? **It is key that outcomes and improvements are disseminated to all teachers**. How are you going to ensure they are going to share their outcomes, their findings – staff meetings? Conference days? An online portal?

Get the balance right between all being equal partners, all being treated with unconditional positive regard and the need for challenge. Teachers will be subject to peer analysis and challenge, and they must be willing to challenge each other.

It is imperative that the observation team explores how students engage with observed lessons. How will you involve students in the process? Will you explore students' work? Will you interview students to inform the post-lesson discussion after observation? Many schools run case studies on key students identified before each Lesson Study period, is this something that could add value to your Lesson Study?

Criteria should be set for the post lesson discussion. Key rules should be in place – teachers must commit to listening to each other fully and build on the discussion, making suggestions, raising questions and at all times being accountable to the lesson aims.

When sharing new practice, knowledge and outcomes with colleagues, each group must commit to doing so as accurately and vividly as possible. Some schools endeavour to do the same with their students, albeit appropriately, depending on their ages and stages of development. Their views and ideas should be treated with equal positive regard.

Agree which class you work with for each research lesson in advance and then identify three students who might represent different groups of learner in the class. Students who are making good, average or below-average progress and students who are disengaged.

Review and modify your teaching materials carefully and write down exactly what you want each pupil to be able to do with their new knowledge by the end of the lesson. **With regard to the technique you are refining or planning, note down what you hope the response of each case student will be. What will each student do at each stage to evidence their progress?**

Identify what resources will be used and how, exactly what you will write on the board, where and when and indicate timings for the lesson stages. **Essentially your aim when planning is to produce a lesson which drives every outcome and meets every need**. You should then agree which member of your team will focus their observation on which case student; it is imperative you don't all gather data on the same student having missed one of the case study students.

You may want to create a lesson observation pro forma with common questions and common points of observation. That is not to say that each observer cannot follow their own thoughts and ideas, but it might be good to have some commonality.

In terms of the class and the case study students, prior to the observation you should explain to them that you are trying to improve their experience so that learning and teaching in the school can improve. Age-appropriately, of course, and maintaining a professional boundary, you may want to explain each part of the process and exactly what Lesson Study is and how you have arrived at an observation.

Observers should zoom in and capture the case students' responses and reactions at different points in the lesson. In the post-observation discussion, the difference between what was observed and what was predicted in the pre-observation discussion should form a hugely important discussion.

More general observations should be made about the lesson and about students generally. Were there any misunderstandings? Miscommunications? **Remember, the point of the observation and the post-observation discussion is to perfect something you already thought close to perfect**. If interviewing students post-observation, or indeed involving them in the post-observation discussions, decide whether to invite them beforehand so that they are prepared or after so that their feedback may be more genuine. Try to capture some of their exact words/phrases in your notes; it can be hugely interesting and telling to note verbatim, the instruction given by the teacher.

In the first round you may wish to invite an external expert, someone experienced in Lesson Study, to observe your planning sessions, your observation and your post-observation discussions so that every stage of the process is reviewed and given the opportunity to be improved. This should not be confused with knowledgeable others, who should be available at every stage. Knowledgeable others play an important role as sources for expert advice as well as facilitating the sharing of ideas between Lesson Study groups when appropriate.

Many schools video the lesson and/or record the sound. Indeed, it would not be uncommon to have a number of cameras running, focusing on the teacher, the entire class and the case study students.

After each cycle of steps (outlined in Figure 6), you should arrange opportunities for members of the lesson study group to work with other teachers to share learning outcomes that have been reached and/or evolved. This work is vital and should take place as close to the end of each cycle as is possible. Articulating improvement and outcomes across your school is paramount in terms of improvement and in terms of increasing buy-in in the early stages of Lesson Study.

Do not get so immersed in the process that you forget to celebrate and value what has been learned and shared. As well as feeding back in groups, at staff meetings and/or conference days, you may want to create an online virtual learning environment (VLE) so that learning outcomes can be reviewed and revisited at any time. Providing you have permission, video can be shared online, as can every stage of the process, thus modelling the Lesson Study process and sharing the improvements and outcomes reached.

You now have a good idea about three major different Professional Development models available to you, and you have the tools to set your chosen model in motion. There remains one final important area to consider: how to evaluate success once your programme has begun. Evaluation will form a key component of your planning and is essential to ensuring that you meet your intended outcomes.

Chapter Three summary

This chapter has introduced you to three models of Professional Development and looked in detail at how to think about implementing them.

1. Coaching

- Step 1: Set up coaching groups
- Step 2: Structure your coaching conversations
- Step 3: Carry out a lesson observation
- Step 4: Carry out a post-observation conversation
- Step 5: Work between observations

2. Taught professional development

- Tier 1: Orientation
- Tier 2: Teaching and Learning
- Tier 3: Educational Leadership
- Tier 4: Master's level and Headship

3. Lesson study

- 1: Form your group
- 2: Identify the focus area
- 3: Research the focus area
- 4: Plan the lesson
- 5: Assign roles and identify case students
- 6: Carry out the lesson
- 7: Discuss evidence from the lesson observation
- 8: Draw conclusions and implement

4   Measuring success

....

Training and development is a substantial investment of both money and time. You need to know the value of Professional Development **programmes, specifically whether or not they are worth pursuing or sustaining. In this section we will look at how to measure and evaluate the success of your programme and identify what outcomes have been achieved.**

....

INTRODUCTION

In order for your Professional Development programme to be a success, you need to be able to answer one fundamental question:

Does your programme deliver benefits to your institution?

This simple question lies at the heart of training evaluation. You need to understand whether the steps you are taking are delivering on the core aims of your programme and in doing so making a positive contribution to your organisation. Those aims should ultimately be to *improve teaching and learning*, and in doing so to *improve student outcomes* in your school, in line with your core principles (see **Chapter One:** *First Steps* for more on core aims and core principles). This section looks at how to identify whether or not you are meeting this objective.

Regardless of how impressive or popular training programmes appear to be, outcomes are what matter and they must be measured in systematic and quantitative terms. This tends to come down to two areas: costs and results. In other words, what is the *return on investment*? Is the cost in terms of time and money worth the result?

For you, the feedback gained from measuring outcomes will allow you to develop your programme, maintain engagement and ensure long-term success. For others, the feedback will determine whether your programme is worth their own ongoing investment, be that in terms of time and effort, or money.

If you are asking people to invest, it is inevitable that they will want to see a system in place that will measure the return on that investment. Consider for example your finance manager, who needs to sign off on the funding for your programme, or your staff member working a 12-hour day in order to attend an after-school Professional Development event that you have scheduled. They will be looking to see evidence that backs up the anticipated outcomes of your programme, not only to justify its value to themselves but also to understand how that value will translate into real-world results.

All staff should be made aware of the basics of the model you choose to use, the importance of carrying out such evaluation and the benefits both to staff and to your school generally.

YOUR SYSTEM OF EVALUATION WILL ALLOW YOU TO:

1. JUSTIFY THE CURRENT INVESTMENT (IN TERMS OF BUDGET AND TIME)
2. SECURE FUNDING GOING FORWARD
3. PROVE THAT THE TIME INVESTED WAS WORTH IT
4. MAKE ADJUSTMENTS IN LIGHT OF FEEDBACK
5. IDENTIFY WHAT YOUR ORGANISATION HAS GAINED
6. DETERMINE COSTS VERSUS BENEFITS OF THAT GAIN

This chapter will look at the following four areas, using the Kirkpatrick model as the foundation for its discussion around measuring and evaluation:

| Going beyond grade scores | The Kirkpatrick model | Developing tools to measure outcomes | Evaluation techniques |

■ **MEASURING IMPACT:** GOING BEYOND GRADE SCORES

You will already have a quantitative measure of success in place at your school: grade scores. Grade scores provide a simple measure of 'success' that can situate student achievement both within your school and on a national scale. But you cannot focus on these alone. There are a number of limitations to using grade scores as a measure of Professional Development success:

- Many factors unrelated to your programme will have an ongoing impact on grade scores, making it impossible for you to isolate the role your programme has played in those results.

- Some of the outcomes you may wish to drive will be subjective – increased confidence, resilience and happiness, for example. These will not be identified in grade scores, which have a very narrow focus for their assessment of success.

- It will take a significant period of time for the benefits of your Professional Development programme to take hold and impact on grade scores. (Indeed, research shows that the most effective programmes which aim to bring about significant organisational and cultural change need at least two terms to take hold, and that one-off events rarely have a significant impact.)

Thinking long-term

Measuring success will need to be more nuanced than simply delivering a course and looking for a percentage increase in grade scores. As **Chapter Two:** *Breaking Down Barriers* identified, Professional Development is only truly effective over the long term, and your methods of evaluation will need to reflect that.

In order to go beyond this simple measure of evaluation, you need to reframe the question that opens this chapter and ask yourself:

How do you want your programme to benefit your institution?

While it may be the case that ultimately schools are in fact judged by graded student outcomes (i.e. their grade scores), there are many ways to bring about a measurable improvement in the culture of your institution, which will then go on to impact on those scores. You must isolate the methods by which you seek to bring about this improvement.

You must also be aware of other factors that could divert attention away from your initiative. In other words, if your school improves, how will you know what improvement can be traced back to your programme? How will you be able to *prove* how and where your initiative had impact? Grade scores may be the final step in assessment but they should not be your sole focus. Your evaluation will need to go deeper.

Aims:

WRITE UP A LIST OF SPECIFIC OUTCOMES THAT YOU WOULD LIKE YOUR PROFESSIONAL DEVELOPMENT PROGRAMME TO MEET. FOR EXAMPLE:

- RAISE CONFIDENCE

- INITIATE BEHAVIOURAL OR CULTURAL CHANGE TO BRING ABOUT A COMPLETELY DIFFERENT APPROACH TO TEACHING

- DRIVE GRADE OUTCOMES

- INCREASE HAPPINESS/SATISFACTION LEVELS

- GROW RESILIENCE IN YOUR STAFF

■ THE KIRKPATRICK MODEL

High-quality training will impact on people in different ways and over different periods of time. This chapter will use the **Kirkpatrick model**, a four-tier model that has come to be recognised as the worldwide standard for assessing the success of training, to understand how to carry out evaluation across this broad spectrum of impact.

The Kirkpatrick model considers the value of any type of training, formal or informal, across four levels. *Level 1* evaluates how participants respond to the training – known as **reaction**. *Level 2* seeks to measure if participants actually learned the material – the **learning** stage. *Level 3* looks at whether participants go on to use and apply what they have learned – the **behaviour** stage. Finally, *Level 4* evaluates whether the training has positively impacted the institution – the **results** stage. The final stage can sometimes be applied simply as a monetary 'return on investment' measure, which tends to be more easily applied in the world of production industry where a more tangible product is produced. Nevertheless, approached with thought,

Tailoring the Kirkpatrick model to education

such a measure can be applied to educational institutions, both in terms of financial investment, and in terms of return on investment of time and effort.

> ### The Kirkpatrick Model
> ....
>
> Donald Kirkpatrick was Professor Emeritus at the University of Wisconsin and was president of the American Society for Training and Development. In 1959 he first published his Four-Level Training Evaluation Model in the *US Training and Development Journal* and updated the model in 1975. Despite the fact that the evaluation model introduced by Kirkpatrick is now over 50 years old, its simple, matter-of-fact approach makes it the most widely used system of evaluation worldwide.

Figure 7: *The Kirkpatrick model[1]*

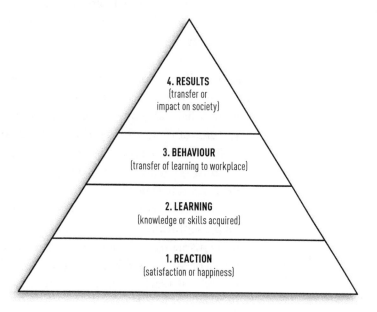

---

1   The original model for this was published in Craig, R.L. (ed.). (1967). *Training and Development Handbook*. New York, NY. McGraw-Hill.

It is worth studying these four tiers in more detail before looking at how to develop tools to carry out this model in practice.

1. Reaction

How are staff *reacting* to your programme? The reaction level measures how your staff have responded to your sessions, in whichever form they make take. It is important to measure reaction, because it helps you understand how well the training is being received by your audience. It also helps you improve the training for future trainees, including identifying important areas or topics that are missing from the training.

Reaction may be measured at the end of every session or after a series of sessions. There are obvious benefits and downsides to both approaches. Whilst your aim is to capture as true a picture as possible, it is important that gathering feedback does not become onerous.

Qualitative versus quantitative measures

Whilst the data may be *qualitative* rather than *quantitative*, and therefore less immediately tangible, you are essentially gauging customer satisfaction first-hand, and for many organisations this should be their most important success criteria.

Gauging reaction from your participants will be different from gauging, say, the reaction from a front-facing customer service situation, since there is a known, pre-existing relationship between the 'supplier' (you) and the 'customer' (your staff). This is even more skewed if your programme is being delivered in-house by your own 'expert' staff but, if the right environment is created – an environment where absolute honestly is valued with carefully thought out systems of review – then the feedback you get will be of benefit.

Realising the value of teaching

The reaction phase is about the immediate response that your training engenders. Obviously, you want your staff to feel that Professional Development is a valuable experience, and you want them to feel positive about the delivery, the topic, the material and its presentation. 'In the moment', your programme has the potential to be inspiring and, therefore, lift people's spirits and motivate them to try harder, as staff are reminded how important and life-changing the role of teacher can be. Training programmes can bring about a greater sense of team spirit and, therefore, bring about greater collaboration amongst staff, which in turn will impact on teaching and learning, and therefore grade scores.

Whilst it is hoped that good-quality Professional Development will be inspiring, it is not usually the primary aim. However, since it is easier to impart Professional Development on those relatively new to teaching (as their skills base is still growing), and since those with a few years under their belt might be more likely to adopt a *what I do already works for me* approach, so the need to win hearts and minds first, is greater. The reaction stage, therefore, is important as a precursor to the learning stage.

Winning hearts and minds

2. Learning

Learning lies at the core of Professional Development. Most Professional Development is primarily devised to:

1. teach new skills,

2. improve knowledge, and therefore

3. improve practice.

How much has knowledge increased?

In order to measure what your trainees have learned, you first need to make clear what it is they are *supposed* to learn, and establish a baseline measure of their prior knowledge. Only then can you truly measure how much their knowledge has increased as a result of the training. It is important to measure this because knowing what your trainees are learning and what they are not will help you improve future training. Ideally, you would have surveyed staff prior to commencing your programme, or prior to each session, in terms of learning needs in order to inform planning.

3. Behaviour

Is knowledge being applied?

The highest order outcome for your Professional Development programme should be to bring about a change in behaviour. Just because people attending your programme are learning and growing their skills base does not necessarily mean they are applying what they have learned. The ultimate goal of Professional Development should be to translate that new learning into a change in behaviour in the classroom or school generally.

Specifically, this stage seeks to evaluate how far your trainees have changed their behaviour based on the training they have received, and it does this by looking at how trainees apply the information learned. However, a lack of change in behaviour does not necessarily mean that your staff have not learned anything. Perhaps their line manager is resistant to allowing them to apply new knowledge or change too much when current methods appear to be delivering results. Or maybe they have learned everything they have been taught by your programme, but they have no desire to apply the knowledge themselves as they perceive that everything is working as-is. Asking people to change behaviour and adopt new practice is a big ask, and can be affected by many factors (revisit **Chapter Two:** *Breaking Down Barriers* for more on possible barriers to change).

4. Results

At this level, you will analyse the final *results* of your training. Unlike the reaction phase, you will not be carrying out this evaluation the day after your last session has been delivered. Results are a longer-term measure, and many weeks or indeed months may pass before you can gauge the full impact of any Professional Development programme. This level also depends on the measures you or your organisation have determined to be good for your school(s), good for the staff, and/or good for your students.

Measuring return on investment

At this final stage, all four measures must be taken together and a decision made around what represents a 'return on investment'. Should it be decided that the programme did not deliver a return on investment, adjustments must be made; the depth of research around the power of Professional Development should reassure you that it is highly unlikely that you decide to abandon your programme altogether. Furthermore, by following the preparation outlined in **Chapters One** to **Three** and indeed this chapter, you should have mechanisms in place that will have flagged up any concerns long before a final conclusion would be drawn that no value was added. The results stage, therefore, should be about taking a look at your programme as a whole, and working out how to continue to refine and perfect it going forward, so that return on investment is guaranteed.

■ DEVELOPING TOOLS TO MEASURE OUTCOMES

In this section we will build the tools that you will need to carry through Kirkpatrick's model.

1: Reaction tool

Your reaction tool will be governed by immediate feedback. You will need to consider questions such as:

- Did the trainees feel that the training was worth their time?
- Did they think that it was successful?
- What were the strengths of the training, and the weaknesses?
- Did they like the venue and presentation style?
- Did the training session meet their personal learning styles?

At this stage you must think about how you are going to address these questions to your staff. A strong approach is to source three different types of feedback: *written*, *verbal* and *observed*. Written feedback could be collected in the form of *evaluation forms*, *learning logs/reflective journals*, *portfolios* and *student surveys*. Verbal feedback can *post-observation interviews* and *focus groups* (see the section on 'Evaluation Techniques', on page 87, for more detail on these).

You should not only survey your trainees but also your Professional Development instructors and your students, to see how they feel each session went.

Direct observation

Finally, carry out direct observations. Watch trainees' body language during training. Is it positive or negative? Once you have carried out your written feedback analysis, ask whether your body language observations have given away any information that confirms or contradicts what your trainees, instructors and students have reported.

Responding to feedback

Once you have gathered this information, examine it closely and begin to evaluate how successful your programme appears to be so far. Throughout the programme you should consider what changes you could make, informed by feedback and suggestions. Ongoing *reaction* analysis is important: do not just wait until the final *results* stage to assess the impact of your programme. This is especially the case if yours is a rolling programme.

2: Learning tool

To measure learning, start by identifying what you want to evaluate. Look for changes in:

- knowledge
- skills
- attitudes

Before/after trainee tests

Conducting ongoing interviews

It is often helpful to measure these areas both before and after training. So, before training commences, test your trainees to determine their prior knowledge and skill levels, and attitudes. Once training is finished, test your trainees a second time to measure how these have developed. Look at what they have learned, or measure learning with interviews or verbal and written assessments – you can use the techniques identified in the next section, 'Evaluation Techniques', just as you did to measure *reaction*, but you will be applying these techniques at the beginning and end of a training course, rather than at the beginnin and end of each class or session.

For example, you might set out a pre-training assessment around questioning that asks your teachers to respond to the following techniques:

Rate your knowledge/skill around the following techniques:	1	2	3	4	5	✔
Blooms Taxonomy	○	○	○	○	○	
Hierarchical questioning	○	○	○	○	○	
Moving questions around the room	○	○	○	○	○	
Using think-pair-share	○	○	○	○	○	

You should then revisit the same questions after training and look for change.

3: Behaviour tool

It can be challenging to measure behaviour effectively. This is a longer-term activity that should take place weeks or months after the initial training.

One of the best ways to measure behaviour is to conduct observations and interviews over time. As a way of evaluating behavioural impact, you could create questionnaires around hands-on takeaways from sessions, skills or techniques that your staff actually intend to use. Asking staff directly how they intend to change their practice can often be the gentle push they need. Before a teaching session, ask your teachers to identify what teaching technique they intend to use. For example, will they:

- pre-write key questions to be asked?
- share pre-written questions before the lesson?
- use the collaborative learning technique 'think-pair-share'?
- ask students to exit the room with a Post-it question?
- begin lessons with the questions from the previous lesson?

This can then be followed up after the session, and then the process repeated some two or three months later, using the same questions – asking first if they carried through on their intention and second asking how effective they found the skill/technique to be. This will allow you to evaluate the effectiveness of your training sessions. Essentially you are asking:

- Did your teachers put any of their learning to use?
- Are teachers able to teach their new knowledge, skills, or attitudes to other people?
- Are teachers aware that they have changed their behaviour?

Remember that behaviour will only change if conditions are favourable. For instance, effective learning could have taken place in the training session, but if the overall organisational culture is not set up for any behaviour changes, the trainees might not be able to apply what they have learned.

Alternatively, trainees might not receive support, recognition or reward for their behaviour change from their boss. So, over time, they disregard the skills or knowledge that they have learned, and go back to their old behaviours. Revisit **Chapter 2** for more on how to manage these potential barriers.

4: Results tool

Of all the levels, measuring the final results of your training programme is likely to be the most difficult and time-consuming. It is also one of the most important, as this is likely to be (at least in part) a quantitative measure that will be used to reassure others of the value of your course and the credibility of its outcomes.

How and when

You should first consider how much time you are going to allow your programme before you expect to see results. If you are going to measure student grade outcomes, when and how would you expect to see an increase?

- In the first year?
- Across all subjects?
- What would constitute success?
- What would constitute return on investment?

The biggest challenge will be identifying which outcomes, benefits or final results are most closely linked to your training, and coming up with an effective way to measure these outcomes over the long term.

Consider the objectives of your training, for example:

- Increasing grade outcomes
- Increasing employee retention
- Raising morale
- Improving staff attitudes to learning and improvement
- Achieving higher quality ratings under inspection
- Improving student/parental satisfaction.

Quantitative measurement

While results such as improved morale amongst staff and students is a qualitative measure and can be identified using similar evaluation techniques to those you will employ for *reaction*, *learning* and *behaviour*, others such as grade outcomes, employee retention and inspection ratings will give you your first quantitative measures. You will need to tie these together to make your case for the longer-term success of of your programme. The following section will equip you with qualitative evaluation techniques to achieve this.

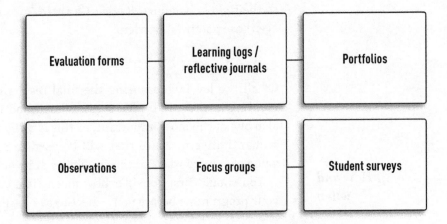

EVALUATION TECHNIQUES

Having identified what you need to consider at each stage of your evaluation process, it is worth looking in more detail at some of the evaluation techniques you will use. The following are applicable, to a greater or lesser extent, across all four stages of your Kirkpatrick model assessment.

■ 1. Evaluation forms

Evaluation forms can be used at Levels 1, 2 and, to an extent, Level 3. Choose between:

- **Multiple-choice questions:** You can construct your questionnaires using simple *yes/no* questions, or you may adopt Likert-style scaled questions (for example, 1 = strongly agree, 5 = strongly disagree). Multiple-choice questions allow for easier measure. However, the answers may return narrow responses which fail to give a full and true picture of knowledge or understanding.

- **Open-ended questions:** Open-ended questions allow for greater comment. They can also be useful if you would like to obtain qualitative information from a large number of people – more than you could possibly interview or invite to participate in focus groups. However, it is harder to review and draw common conclusions from the answers.

- **A combination of both:** This might be suitable if it makes the process more accessible. As with so much, balance is key.

Remember, the most important question on a questionnaire is about the suitability of the questionnaire: 'Was this questionnaire helpful/fit for purpose?'

Using online assistants

Take time when constructing your questionnaires so that questions you ask are precise. Your participants should know exactly what you want to find out. If you are conducting online surveys, you may want to use an online assistant such as Survey Monkey or create a Google Forum. Using this system, participants can fill out surveys online and you can receive collated results instantly.

Rather than developing your own questionnaire, you may prefer to find one that has already been developed that has reliability and validity data to support it. Online you will find a number of questionnaires around areas such as school culture, enthusiasm for teaching, job satisfaction and attitudes. These can provide a solid foundation to your questioning but are best when adapted to suit your institution.

- During **Level 1: Reaction**, your staff should respond to questions about the content, process and context of the training. You are looking at how your trainees are responding to sessions, but it is important that your evaluation forms should not just operate as 'happy sheets', assessing whether your trainees are having a good time. This level of evaluation should essentially ask if the session has met the stated objectives. Did the participants feel it was worthwhile?

  At the *reaction* level, evaluations should take place immediately after each session, or within a short space of time. The short time-span means that what participants are able to evaluate is their actual reaction to the event, rather than the effect the event has had on their practice.

- At the **Level 2: Learning** stage, evaluation forms can be used to assess what new knowledge staff have gained from the Professional Development session(s). Your staff should complete them at the end of the training course or very soon afterwards to record what they have learned.

  Gauging prior knowledge

  You may need to conduct pre-event questionnaires in order to gauge prior knowledge. As mentioned earlier, the fact that someone claims not to have learned anything from a session does not mean the session was not fit for purpose; it may be that the session was not fit for *their* purpose specifically. Each trainee will have different needs, and fine-tuning your Professional Development sessions will allow you to meet as many of those needs as possible.

- At **Level 3: Behaviour**, evaluation forms can be used, but they are not the best measure to gauge behavioural changes, because behavioural change tends to happen over time. More effective to measure this are learning logs or reflective journals.

See also *student surveys* on page 91 for guidance on using evaluation forms with your students.

2. Learning logs / reflective journals

Open-ended reflection

Personal logs and journals give your trainees more freedom with their feedback, but you should still provide guidelines as to what form these journals should take. These can be structured around open-ended questions and areas to address so that participants are looking at the same issues. This means that you, or whoever is evaluating them, can easily compare what each person has recorded.

> **Learning logs and reflective journals are highly effective as the process of reflecting on behavioural change can become a 'self-fulfilling prophecy'.**

By forcing people to examine closely just how much their approach to their role has changed, or indeed by making them realise how fixed they are in their mindset, you can often jump-start people towards greater levels of experimentation and risk-taking.

3. Portfolios

Formally recording learning

Participants can keep portfolios of their work to demonstrate how they have incorporated what they have learned into their practice. Again, the process of asking them to formally record how they have applied what they have learned is very powerful as a means for participants to demonstrate to themselves just how much they have developed. The owner of the portfolio can choose what to include, or the items to include can be listed at the start of a term or semester.

Portfolios generally include rubrics so that the entries can be assessed. The assessor of the portfolio is able to see the participant's progress over time.

People who put their portfolios together will spend a great deal of time doing so, so they will need to see the value of their efforts. In return, therefore, the person who is assessing portfolios will need to spend a significant amount of time going through them and giving quality feedback.

Teacher portfolios could include items such as:

- lesson plans
- information about how they have implemented what they learned in their professional development
- videos of lessons they have taught.

It is often helpful to invite people to write a reflection on what they learned from putting their portfolios together, which in itself is an evaluation of their learning overall.

Evaluation at this level moves from the immediate *reaction* of the participants (Level 1) – whether they enjoyed the session – to what the participants have learned as a result of the event (level 2 on-wards). What do they know now, that they did not know before? What skills have they gained?

You must create a system that moves candidates away from:

'I learned this, we did that,'

To:

'I learned this and it will have that effect on my practice,'

'We did this, and because we did, this happened (or will happen).'

Evaluation at this level is looking not only at the event, but at the effect that event has had. The focus of evaluation shifts to the participant as 'practitioner' rather than merely as a learner only.

4. Observations

Non-judgemental assessment

Direct observations can be quite intimidating and often come with the fear of judgement. Should you choose to use direct observation to gauge learning, it must be made clear that any observation is focusing only on the skills studied in the session. It would also make sense to carry out colleague-to-colleague observation in order to remove any link to performance management.

Observers should watch each other to see how they are implementing their new skills in the classroom. Some observations could be filmed so that all parties are involved in the review or evaluation. Observers could look for behaviours in students that would be expected as a result of the teacher's implementation of what they have learned.

Do not assume that everyone is able to observe effectively. Observers may need to be trained in what to look for. They should do their best not to intrude and should observe at times when they will see what they want to observe.

Self-observation | Self-observation is an important part of the daily working life of teaching staff. Reflective practitioners are constantly assessing their own work, both while they are teaching (e.g. 'Why isn't this class responding?') and as a reflective exercise after teaching (e.g. 'That went well / That didn't go as expected / What can I do next time to change it?'). Peer observation takes place as an extended part of professional discussion – it is an arrangement between members of teaching staff to observe each other, and then discuss the results of those observations.

Observations should be based on the built trust between the participants. At its best it should be experienced as a supportive part of the life of the school and of each participant's professional development.

5. Focus groups

Focus groups may lead out of a series of observations involving many staff. In a focus group, participants interact with each other to share their thoughts and feelings about a particular topic or theme.

Ideas sharing | Generally, it is good to have between five and seven people in a focus group; you will at least need more than two or three in order to have group synergy. On the other hand, if you have too many participants, it is harder for individual thoughts and feelings to be fully considered because so many will be trying to make their thoughts heard at once.

It may be a good idea to nominate a note-taker to document the group discussion. This will allow evaluation to take place, but it must also be made clear that no judgements about performance will be made as a result of those notes. You may wish to supply a standard *pro froma* or set of questions to the group so they can evaluate the success of a particular session or series of sessions as a collective.

6. Student surveys

Including students | Identify the student group most likely to benefit from the content of the session or sessions. Put together a short survey for these students that relates to the particular areas covered by the session.

Tip: How to use your students in assessment

Since one of your main aims should be to improve your students' experience at your institution, it is a good idea to involve them in the process. **If you need a mechanism to measure change in behaviour in the classroom, then your greatest resource should be your students.** Some schools have involved students in observations, having set clear boundaries and conducted training, to great success.

You can also put in place **360-degree reviews** using peers, students and those delivering your Professional Development programme. A '360-degree' review is a tool that allows a number of people to be involved in an evaluation process. Rather than just relying on the individual to reflect on their perceived behaviour change, all involved feed into the review process, thus creating a truer picture.

Evaluation at this level shifts the focus yet again – this time away from the practitioner and onto peers and students. To effectively evaluate the impact of Professional Development at this level, the focus of reflection must not rest entirely with the practitioner. Without this final link in the chain, the Professional Development cycle is incomplete, because there is no way of seeing the final outcome.

When preparing your student survey, think about whether to use closed or open-ended questions – or both. Before a course on feedback, for example, an open-ended question might be:

What form of feedback do you find most useful for improving your work and why?

Alternatively, for a classroom management skills course, a closed question might gather useful quantifiable data about the number of times students feel their learning has been disrupted in the past four or five lessons.

After the course, having given candidates time to implement your learning from the day, revisit the survey you gave to students. Ask them to complete it again, making any small changes as necessary. Compare the two data sets to identify any changes that have taken place, and consider the extent to which this matches your expectations. If your survey does not reveal which changes to staff practice have had the biggest impact on students, you might consider supplementing the survey with some short pupil interviews. Over time you may choose to repeat the survey/interview process at intervals, to ensure your direct, positive impact is well targeted.

Chapter Four summary

This chapter has used the Kirkpatrick model to create customised tools to measure the success of your Professional Development programme.

1. **Measuring impact: Going beyond grade scores**
   - Introducing qualitative impact measures

2. **The Kirkpatrick model**
   - Reaction (satisfaction or happiness)
   - Learning (knowledge or skills acquired)
   - Behaviour (transfer of learning to workplace)
   - Results (transfer or impact on society)

3. **Developing tools to measure outcomes**
   - Reaction tool
   - Learning tool
   - Behaviour tool
   - Results tool

4. **Evaluation techniques**
   - Evaluation forms
   - Learning logs / reflective journals
   - Portfolios
   - Observations
   - Student surveys

Real-world example:
Parkside Federation Academies, UK

....

In order to understand what the practical advice in this book looks like in real terms, what follows is an example of the way in which a group of schools in the UK identified and addressed the Professional Development needs of their teachers.

Parkside Federation Academies (PFA), a Multi-Academy Trust, had in place a limited Professional Development offer that primarily catered for new staff by putting them through induction training. PFA identified a need to develop that offer and to provide support and training for staff throughout their career, across all five schools within the Trust.

....

BACKGROUND

Parkside Federation Academies (PFA) is a Multi-Academy Trust consisting of five schools across Cambridge, UK. PFA is made up of Parkside Community College in the heart of the city; Coleridge Community College, at the centre of a community district of Cambridge; Trumpington Community College, at the centre of a recently built community district of Cambridge; University Technical College Cambridge (UTCC), a science specialist college in Cambridge; and Parkside Sixth, an International Baccalaureate specialist sixth form college in the heart of Cambridge. The Trust has a maximum student number of 2500 across all schools but is not at full capacity, as Trumpington is newly built and UTCC is expanding. PFA has a reputation of delivering outstanding education and as a brand it represents quality in education, holding to its core values of excellence, innovation and collaboration. Indeed, its flagship school, Parkside Community College, is rated 'Outstanding' on inspection and is in the top 5% of schools nationally in the UK.

Figure 8: *Parkside Federation Academies structure*

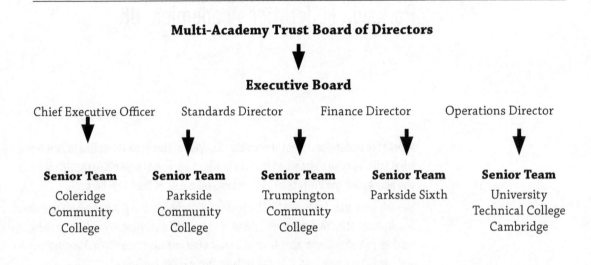

CONTEXT

Parkside Federation Academies experienced a high turnover of staff, greater than institutions of a similar size. When exploring reasons for this it became apparent that in terms of continuing Professional Development training, staff new to the Trust were catered for in terms of induction, but beyond that the offer tended to be somewhat ad hoc. A cultural change was needed so that all staff at all stages of the profession were catered for. As well as adhering to this moral obligation to develop staff, the need to develop and grow their own talent was also great. The Trust's plans for growth would see a number of leadership positions being created, yet there was not a natural pool of staff to fill these positions.

Solutions to staffing issues were often reactive or relied on luck, with very little future proofing in place across the Trust. Huge investments were made to hire new staff. Significant financial investment was also made into advertising, the time taken to interview new staff, and then a year-long induction package involving a mentor and a number of taught sessions, only to find that 30% of staff moved on after less than three years. More by luck than judgement, key roles – such as examination officer, data manager and timetabling officer as well as teaching staff responsible for key faculty areas – were filled by staff who had been within the Trust long term. But, increasingly, the senior leadership team were becoming concerned about how they might cope with an exodus of staff from these key positions.

Four years ago such an exodus occurred and a little over 30% of staff resigned, leaving some departments decimated. Examination of exit interviews showed that a number staff were moving on to promoted positions outside of the Trust that arguably they were not ready for. Due to a shortage of staff within the teaching profession UK-wide, some schools are willing to promote staff early and develop them in-role; whilst this can be very successful, it can also lead to people leaving the profession burnt out and disenfranchised.

Exit interviews also showed that many staff who had joined a flagship organisation expected far greater staff development and training. This cemented the belief that something had to be done to build a true and deep culture of staff development. One of the directors was charged with the job, starting with teaching staff. What was paramount was that from the outset the Trust's executive board and senior leadership teams of each school knew that this was not going to be an overnight fix.

THE PROCESS: LARGE-SCALE QUESTIONS

During the first stages of the consultation process, the executive board and senior leadership teams looked at large-scale questions before adopting a more granular approach. The first job was to consider the current offer and to work out what was working and what needed to be cut. This was not as simple as looking at attendance figures, as there are a number of factors influencing why people do and do not attend. The induction package, for example, was often written into staff appraisal and therefore linked to the following year's pay increase. Likewise, some courses were scheduled on a day of the week that a number of people could not attend as their teaching timetable meant they were unable to.

One unfair aspect of the appraisal system was that it was pretty ad hoc as to whether pay was linked to engagement in Professional Development; it very much came down to the appraiser's approach rather than policy. It became clear that, like a lot of institutions, systems had been laid down over time and some were no longer fit for purpose. The same could be said for the training on offer. A new data system had been in place for two years and yet no training had been devised and offered – staff, however, were still expected to engage with the new system.

As a starting point, an imaginary *what would we do if we were starting afresh* set of criteria was drawn up. There was a statutory obligation to offer a specific induction package for newly qualified teachers joining the Trust. There was clearly a need for a systems-based induction package regardless of career point. Further, there was a need to develop teachers into the very best classroom practitioners focusing on excellent teaching. The next stage was to develop a package that would develop staff through different career paths. This needed to be a package that would focus on educational leadership as well as providing a route through to senior management in preparation for Headship. A decision would need to be made about the level of each package and whether staff would be taken to Master's level.

After further consultation with the executive board and senior team, a point was raised about the need for one-off standalone courses – for example, a newly qualified teacher (NQT) following NQT Induction might need or indeed want to access a course on Effective Group Work or Interactive Learning. Another point was raised about the need for more specific, intense support for teachers struggling with a particular aspect of their practice. Both these considerations were also pertinent for staff who had chosen to not engage fully with a specific pathway in a particular year but might have wanted some professional learning.

The decision was made therefore to seek to devise courses that would adhere as a whole, but would also be made up of sessions that would stand alone. For example, the Excellence in Learning and Teaching course would consider excellent teaching in all its component parts. Teachers could therefore access the entire course or attend one session or a selection of sessions. A final large-scale consideration was what would be offered Trust-wide and what would be school-specific. This decision would be based on a number of factors, some political in terms of building *esprit de corps* at school level, as well as meeting the specific needs of each school site.

NEWLY QUALIFIED TEACHER INDUCTION

In the UK there are a strict set of rules governing the induction of an NQT. During their year-long induction period they must be given a reduced timetable. They must also be assigned a mentor and they must meet regularly with that mentor. Beyond the mentor there must be a senior member of staff with ultimate responsibility for their induction and they must have access to this person should a problem arise beyond their mentor's remit. This also provides a safety net should the problem be the relationship with their mentor. During the induction period regular assessments must be made against the UK Teacher Standards. Invariably, these are observations of their teaching and discussion around evidence to support the meeting of teacher standards.

As NQTs were also seen as new staff, there were core elements of the new staff induction that would become a part of the NQT Induction. The taught session on Use of Data for example would be much needed as would be Safeguarding Children. Other sessions would not be needed or appropriate at the early stages of a teacher's career, sessions such as Running a School Trip or Appraising other Staff. A plan was considered to replace these 'unneeded' sessions with sessions more appropriate for an NQT. It soon became apparent, however, that the desire to thoroughly meet the needs of all staff with this new, bespoke approach, had the potential to become a drain on resources in itself. Aligning courses logistically would be paramoun – for example, aligning sessions from the Excellence in Learning and Teaching pathway appropriate to NQTs with the *gaps* in the NQT Induction pathway. Other ways to reduce the pull on resources would need to be considered and at this point there was a need to pause for thought.

PAUSE FOR THOUGHT

In their desire to build the finest, bespoke continuing Professional Development package on the planet, PFA had to find a balance. Literally, they needed to balance their books, in the face of harsh funding cuts in the UK. If sessions were being run by experienced staff, they had to be sure not to ask too much of a few and risk a hit on morale just as they tried to raise it.

Time is always a factor and there are only so many days in a week. Aligning Professional Development to each school calendar and then the Trust calendar was going to be a challenge. And even if everything could fit logistically, it was paramount that the proposed model was run through every permutation, taking into account NQTs, ambitious teachers striving for excellence, or middle and senior leaders with their eyes on future Headship, to ensure not only that the programme worked, but that it was manageable.

NEW STAFF INDUCTION

When examined closely, it was found that the majority of Professional Development already on offer in terms of New Staff Induction was very much needed. By surveying staff in their second year with the Trust however, it became clear that there was an issue with timing. For example:

> Staff attended a session on the systems and processes needed for organising and running a trip in early October. While feedback reported that the session was well delivered, when the time eventually came for staff to organise a trip, much of the session had become a distant memory. Although the session had been of good quality, staff felt that the session was a bit of a waste of time. When this was married with the fact that the same members of staff had delivered all of the sessions for the last few years running, it became clear that attention to this aspect of Professional Development was much needed.

A series of online training sessions were developed. This meant that staff would be able to access the training exactly when they needed to and were given the autonomy to only attend the sessions needed; to continue the example, there would be no point attending a session on running a trip if you were never going to run a trip. It also meant the staff creating and delivering each session need only do so once. The resources needed were already created, and the filming and uploading of the session was handled by the IT department. The IT department greeted this positively as it was somewhat more creative than the day-in day-out troubleshooting of IT problems that they usually encountered.

The online system automatically tracks who has attended each course. The system is also designed to ensure full attendance – in other words, those 'attending' (i.e. following the online video session) are unable to skip forward through the video presentation; they must view it in full. All the online sessions created that have resources also have instructions to download or print beforehand. What is in place now is a bespoke online induction package that staff can access at their convenience. At the start of the year, during their appraisal meeting, new staff discuss the online core elements they will attend. They are then free to fit that attendance around their own schedules and at the most opportune moment of the academic year. Staff can also revisit sessions should they need to, and could do so alongside a task. The earlier example of planning a trip, or others such as completing risk assessment or accessing specifics of data management systems, proved much more effective with an online tutorial as a guide as opposed to a twilight session several months back.

EXCELLENCE-LEVEL QUALIFICATIONS

The excellence level required the most careful consideration. At this level the most significant amount of growth or development would take place. Whatever this stage was going to look like, the objective was to take 'average' teachers to 'good' and 'good' teachers to 'outstanding'. The same was needed in terms of leadership – this level was to take people with the potential to lead change and realise that potential.

It was imperative that what was to be offered had currency, preferably recognised certification, whilst also being tailored to the needs of a growing Multi-Academy Trust (MAT); not an easy set of criteria to fulfil. After exploring a number of Professional Development providers who appeared to promise excellence in almost everything in an impossibly short amount of time, it became clear that nothing 'off the shelf' would fit. A change of direction was needed and so an outline for the perfect course was created. This was born out of discussion, surveying staff and looking closely at institutional needs both in terms of the classroom and leading outside of the classroom. This came easily, which, paradoxically, was a frustration in that precisely what was needed turned out to be clear and the expertise to create and deliver such courses was already in the MAT. There was a frustration regarding the lack of currency and the lack of portability, but some discussion was had as to whether this was a sacrifice worth making in order to create precisely what was needed. Determined to have all needs met, the search was on for a way to create and deliver personalised courses and gain certificated recognition.

Cambridge International Professional Development Qualifications (PDQs) seemed to be a perfect fit. Through gaining accreditation as a PDQ Centre, courses could be written around a framework provided by Cambridge International but with the content completely open to the Trust's own needs. Courses could be written to recognised certificate and diploma level, and successful candidates could submit a portfolio to be certificated by Cambridge International. PFA was extremely happy to forge a partnership with Cambridge International as it was possible to personalise training internally, while the Cambridge International certification offered a globally recognised mark of quality.

Whilst a considerable body of work was completed and this is a simplified overview, ultimately a programme leader was appointed from within the Trust and PFA became the first accredited PDQ Centre in the UK. Courses were written at certificate and diploma level in Learning and Teaching, and Educational Leadership. After these courses were piloted with staff, strategic conversations were had with some key staff members: those with potential to be the next leaders or excellent teachers and who were also seen as high status or influential amongst the larger body of staff. In the first year uptake was excellent, with over 20 members of staff signing onto the courses. Such high uptake was very pleasing and also cemented the notion that staff were crying out for Professional Development and Learning. This closed the loop and made the entire project seem justified and worthwhile.

It is also important to note that the Educational Leadership qualifications were designed to encompass support staff as well as teachers, as an early commitment was made to develop support staff equal to teaching staff, an issue which had been contentious historically. Pleasingly, this message had been communicated successfully and support staff became a part of the pilot scheme, for the first time sitting side by side with teaching staff in the classroom. This was an enormous cultural shift.

Having linked to Cambridge International, the Trust was able to utilise the relationship they had with University College London (UCL). Another benefit of the Cambridge International PDQ qualifications was that the diploma was recognised by UCL as an entrance-level qualification for their higher-level qualifications. The Trust negotiated with UCL and they are set to offer a UCL Master's programme at PFA delivered by UCL staff. The beauty of the Master's programme is that it is *modular*. There are core modules, but the more open research modules mean that both support staff and teaching staff can access the qualification. It also means that research can focus on classroom practice for those following research into Learning and Teaching. Likewise, Headship can be pursued with research focusing on leading change across the school or Trust. Support staff wanting to reach Director of Operations level can pursue research into leading operational change.

PERSONAL DEVELOPMENT PLANS

Personal Development Plans (PDPs) were put in place to support those in need of support. This applied firstly to the increasing number of unqualified teachers employed within the Trust; that is, teachers with university degrees but no formal teaching education. PDPs were also devised as a mechanism to support teacher under-performance identified through observations. Essentially, PDPs are a supportive process to correct under-performance without having to resort to a more formal route. Through discussion, teachers are assigned a coach to meet with, and they carry out research and observations of others in order to gain insight into how an element of their practice found wanting can be improved.

Conceptually, PDPs are much needed and this process was sensitively thought through, allowing the teacher at the heart of the process as much autonomy as possible. The difficulty when developing any system of this type is that people can greet it negatively for obvious reasons. Another factor, however, was that it replaced a much more harsh and somewhat judgemental process with many negative associations. It is worth noting that it will always be difficult to re-package such a system. To some extent, no matter how sensitively such a system is packaged, branded and named, it is what it is – a mechanism to correct under-performance.

INDIVIDUAL PROFESSIONAL DEVELOPMENT

Whilst research demonstrates that long-term, sustained Professional Development has the greatest impact, there is still an occasional need for individual programmes. Standalone one-off sessions such as Health and Safety training, Science technicians attending COSHH (Control of Substances Hazardous to Health) training and Safeguarding training was, of course, worked into the process. Specialist Professional Development is also needed on occasion, for example, for those wishing to pursue a career in Special Educational Needs or as a Specialist Leader in Education, or equivalent. Such bespoke training is usually provided by external experts and the Trust made sure to investigate the myriad options beforehand rather than waiting until an individual raised the question. This was important in terms of sending the message that all avenues had been considered. It also removed the element of surprise in terms of cost and held the promise of increased staff retention by allowing all training routes to be accessed within the Trust.

SYSTEMS TO SUPPORT

Alongside the revamp of the Trust's Professional Development offer was a revamp of the systems to support. Everything needed to be of quality, and there was little point in having quality courses if people could not book onto them or didn't know which room to go to. Administrative time was assigned to the entire Professional Development system and a clear structure was drawn up so that responsibilities were clear. Logistically, sessions and events had to be *calendared* so that portfolio or essay submissions were staggered so as not to overburden the system.

The *appraisal system* needed to be revamped to include the new pathways. Increasingly, pay progression is linked to skills and outcomes achieved, which are of course linked to professional development, albeit not directly. It was imperative therefore that the Trust's appraisal systems were clear to use and fit for purpose, allowing for staff and line managers to easily select and plan a career pathway linked to engaging with Professional Development. The adapted appraisal system had *points of reflection* built in at key review times, with a full and final evaluation taking place during end-of-year review. It was imperative that the quality of the pathway be reviewed but, more importantly, that the pathway was relevant. Whilst quality is paramount, impact was needed in terms of the individual, the school and the Trust as a whole.

All too often, once the hard work has been done, especially if it is a lot of hard work, the assumption is made that there is no more to be done. However, listening and reacting to feedback is essential in terms of continued buy-in and value. The need for effective review would also inform any future decision to develop site-specific Professional Development systems or pathways. As a forward-looking MAT seeking to grow and expand, the need for diversity would increase, especially if schools or colleges cross-phase were brought into the MAT. Whilst some common Professional Development courses will always be needed and common systems can be employed, the needs of kindergarten or primary schools differ greatly to post-16 institutions.

Reviewing impact in terms of cost is also very important. The cost for Cambridge International PDQs was minimal as the course was run using in-house expertise, but there is an administrative cost upon submission of each portfolio. The Master's programme was costlier and so numbers had to be limited, and a transparent set of criteria had to be drawn up in terms of who accessed the programme and when. This made the need for a clear and effective appraisal system that was fit for purpose even greater.

NEXT STEPS

Two years down the road, having internally reviewed the new pathways programmes, external review was needed; it can be very easy to be impressed by your own creation so it is always good to take a step back and get an unbiased view. A recognised and respected organisation within the UK was asked to carry out a thorough review of the Professional Development provision within each school and across the Trust as a whole. External verification and review is hugely important, not just for reporting to the board of directors but also for ensuring all bases are covered and all future plans fits for purpose. The feedback was both pleasing and beneficial, mainly because it confirmed what the Executive Board already knew in terms of future plans.

Figure 9: *Piecing together the programme*

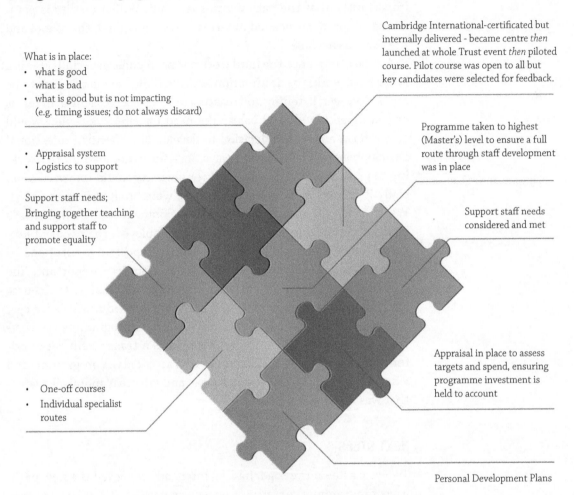

Cambridge International-certificated but internally delivered - became centre *then* launched at whole Trust event *then* piloted course. Pilot course was open to all but key candidates were selected for feedback.

What is in place:
- what is good
- what is bad
- what is good but is not impacting
  (e.g. timing issues; do not always discard)

Programme taken to highest (Master's) level to ensure a full route through staff development was in place

- Appraisal system
- Logistics to support

Support staff needs;
Bringing together teaching and support staff to promote equality

Support staff needs considered and met

- One-off courses
- Individual specialist routes

Appraisal in place to assess targets and spend, ensuring programme investment is held to account

Personal Development Plans

Whilst reviewing current provision, reworking and improving, the biggest job of work to come is creating an equivalent system for support staff. Being able to access the educational leadership pathway and Master's programme is very good start, but the Trust is keenly aware that it needs to create a bespoke pathway for support staff. This must be put in place alongside a performance-related pay system in order to reward support staff in the same manner as teaching staff.

The online New Staff Induction programme is designed for both teaching and support staff and the Master's programme is also fit for support staff, and whilst the Educational Leadership programme can be accessed by all, a bespoke package to enable support staff to be more effective in their role is needed. The Operations Director will take a lead on surveying staff and mapping any provision against the business plan to ensure the balance is struck between meeting the needs of the staff and those of the institution.

Currently the Trust is exploring the commercial possibilities of their pathway programmes. With an increasing need to generate revenue from any stream, externally marketing the Learning and Teaching, and Educational Leadership packages is being explored with partner schools. The challenge of needing to generate income and cut costs is universal, and it may be that other institutions just don't have the money to spend. A more realistic prospect being explored is a one-off Professional Development course outlining how schools can recreate their own package, with lessons learned and guidance given.

•

Like all strong and well thought-out initiatives, the Trust worked to maximise outcomes from the outset. The primary aim was of course to improve outcomes through a culture of professional learning. There was, however, a real need to develop and grow staff, both out of a duty to the staff themselves and to reduce high staff turnover. Along the way it became clear that there were divisions in provision for teaching and support staff and so opportunities were taken to bring together these two aspects of the Trust.

The biggest lesson learned was that you cannot ignore your staff's needs and that people want to be developed and are not made happy by wages alone. Other lessons were around planning for launch and planning logistically so that any new initiative would be held up by the structures around it. Time, money and energy needed to be assigned and roles and responsibilities needed to be made clear.

A good analogy to apply is taking the classroom as a model for greater institutional structures. There is an ongoing need to be clear, to constantly reflect and check on learning, to cater for the needs of all so that all are engaged, and to keep quality at the forefront of all planning – with just enough fun thrown in for good measure.[1]

---

1   This is just one example of the way in which a group of schools chose to address the Professional Development needs of their teachers. Every school is different and every context brings with it different challenges. With this in mind, Cambridge International publishes a range of resources, articles and case studies on their web site: http://www.cambridgeinternational.org/teaching-and-learning/ to support the Professional Development of teachers.

Conclusion

A supportive, collaborative culture in schools is created, not born. It is the result of the way people are encouraged to work together within a given set of circumstances.

The ultimate goal of Professional Development in schools is change in the classroom to bring about a better experience for your students, leading to better outcomes, in every sense.

For Professional Development to be effective, the culture in your institution must be a supportive one, able not only to assimilate but embrace change. Continuing Professional Development for your staff should be about more than just refreshing their knowledge and skills. The cultivation of the culture in your organisation should be the most important aim of your programme and the key building block for the life of your school as a learning community.

Teachers are not merely a collection of skills, nor merely a means of dispensing knowledge. Teacher resilience, motivation and commitment are key factors in the teaching and learning environment of any school.

The core of a school is found in its values.

A school is ultimately defined by its values. Determining those values is a primary responsibility of the leadership team, and placing continuous professional learning at the heart of the institution sets the tone and builds those values. The primary function of a school is to educate, and defining learning as a lifelong pursuit for all through investing fully in Professional Development sets the tone. The organisational culture of each school is different, but lifelong learning for all should be a value that permeates every school the world over.

Collaboration is key

Your job is to facilitate collaboration and remove any barriers to it. A pitfall of peer-led Professional Development is that teachers who are reluctant to change may concede that it works for their colleague, but feel that it is not applicable to their own subject area. Few excellent teaching strategies are subject-specific. Cross-subject collaboration is a powerful and empowering process within staff training. While it is easy to list stereotypical differences between teachers of Literature and Science, or Art and Maths, Professional Development needs to break down these illusory barriers. It is by recognising differences and demonstrating how techniques can be shared and adapted that such barriers can be taken down – albeit slowly and carefully. The last thing you want in a training session is for all the Science teachers or all the History teachers to sit together in a group. They will want to; they may even resent you for it, but it is important for you to resist that pressure and mix them up.

Naturally, teacher-driven training and joint working need not be confined to a single school. There are great examples of sharing excellent in-house training across schools or multi-academy trusts. You may find yourself contending with fear and apprehension amongst some members of staff. Where self-esteem is low, teachers can be reluctant to believe that they can take on board new ideas. Understandably, but self-defeatingly, they prefer to stick to what they know – even if it isn't all that good.

At the heart of schools is learning and teaching, and teachers need to be equipped to teach through their own learning.

Professional Development need not cost the earth, it need not break the bank. All schools have a wealth of expertise and pockets of excellence. Your job is to find this expertise, this excellence, and spread it. Your job is to build a culture of confidence through collaboration, a culture in which teachers remember why they do what they do: to reignite the fire that drove each member of your staff to work in the profession they have chosen. Teachers and support staff might sometimes complain about their working conditions, about a lack of resources or about being overworked. Remember, this is often followed up by a statement about why they continue to do what they do; why they love their job.

> **A mantra of the modern world is around people *working not harder but smarter* and your institution should aim to demonstrate what this means.**

How many institutions give hard and fast examples of such practice and encourage people to do so? Working long, hard days has become the norm in many schools and the misconception that *'those who are last to leave are the ones who really care'* can take hold. As contentious as this may sound, it may be that those people working late are just not equipped to manage their time well. Your Professional Development programme should aim to remedy that.

> **Whilst it may sound as though Professional Development is being sold as a fix-all, the fact is that to some extent this is true.**

Professional Development should teach new skills for the classroom but it should also teach new skills applicable outside the classroom that will in turn make activity inside the classroom more effective. It should show people how to work smarter rather than harder, it should build collaboration in order to facilitate the sharing of skills and of resources. Above all, it should encourage people to reflect on their practice, lay out in front of them a range of skills and strategies, and give them the confidence and desire to be better at what they do.

Bibliography

Allison, S., & Tharby, A. (2015). *Making every lesson count: Six principles to support great teaching and learning*. Crown Horse Publishing.

Archer, J., Cantrell, S., Holtzman, S. L., et al. (2016).*Better feedback for better teaching: A practical guide to improving classroom observations*. Jossey Bass.

Bambrick-Santoyo, & P. Peiser, B. (2012). *Leverage leadership: A practical guide to building exceptional schools*. Jossey Bass.

Barber, B., & Mourshed, M. (2007). *How the world's best-performing school systems come out on top*. McKinsey.

Christodoulou, D. (2017). *Making good progress? The future of assessment for learning*. Oxford University Press.

Damasio, A. (2012). *Self comes to mind: Constructing the conscious brain*. Vintage.

DeWitt, P. M. (2014). *Flipping leadership doesn't mean reinventing the wheel*. Corwin.

Didau, D., & Rose, N. (2016). *What every teacher needs to know about psychology*. John Catt Educational.

Dweck, C. S. (2007). *Mindset: The new psychology of success*. Ballantine.

Hattie, J. (2012). *Visible learning for teachers*. Routledge.

Hattie, J. (2013). *Visible learning and the science of how we learn*. Routledge.

Mccrea, P. (2015). *Lesson observation feedback book: An essential resource for any teacher interested in getting better (High Impact Teaching)*. Create Space Independent Publishing Platform.

Reimers, F. M., & Chung, C. K. (2016). *Teaching and learning for the twenty-first century: Educational goals, policies, and curricula from six nations*. Harvard Education Press.

Smith, A. (2003). *Accelerated learning: A user's guide*. Network Educational Press.

Smith, A. (2011). *High performers: The secrets of successful schools*. Crown House.

William, D. (2016). *Leadership for teacher learning: Creating a culture where all teachers improve so that all students succeed*. Learning Sciences International.

Wiliam, D. (2017). *Embedded formative assessment: Strategies for classroom assessment that drives student engagement and learning*. Solution Tree Press.

Willingham, D. T. (2010). *Why don't students like school?: A cognitive scientist answers questions about how the mind works and what it means for the classroom*. Jossey Bass.

Index